THE MEDIA, THE PRESIDENT, AND PUBLIC OPINION
A Longitudinal Analysis of the Drug Issue, 1984–1991

THE MEDIA, THE PRESIDENT, AND PUBLIC OPINION
A Longitudinal Analysis of the Drug Issue, 1984–1991

William J. Gonzenbach
The University of Alabama

Routledge
Taylor & Francis Group

NEW YORK AND LONDON

First Published by
Lawrence Erlbaum Associates, Inc., Publishers
10 Industrial Avenue
Mahwah, New Jersey 07430

Transferred to Digital Printing 2009 by Routledge
270 Madison Avenue New York, NY 10016
2 Park Square Milton Park, Abingdon Oxon OX14 4RN

Cover design by Kevin Kall

Library of Congress Cataloging-in-Publication Data

Gonzenbach, William, J.
The media, the president, and public opinion : a longitudinal
analysis of the drug issue, 1984–1991 / William J. Gonzenbach.
p. cm.
Includes bibliographical references and index.
ISBN 0-8058-1689-5 (acid-free paper).—ISBN 0-8058-1690-9
1. Drug abuse—Governement policy—United States—Public
opinion. 2. Narcotics, Control of—United States—Public opinion.
3. Public opinion—United States. 4. Drugs and mass media—United
States. 5. Presidents—United States 6. United States—Politics and
government—1981–1991. 7. United States—Politics and government—1989– I. Title.
HV5825.G623 1996
362.29'12'097309048—dc20   95-20856
                                                              CIP

Publisher's Note
The publisher has gone to great lengths to ensure the quality of this reprint
but points out that some imperfections in the original may be apparent.

Contents

Preface

The objective of this book is to examine the drug issue from mid-1984 to mid-1991 with a broadened conceptualization of agenda setting to determine how drug-related issues and events, both real and fabricated, and the primary agendas drove the issue over time. Four questions are examined based on this objective. First, how did the media structure interpretations of drug issues and events? Second, how did the president structure public relations interpretations and presentations of issue and event information over time? Third, what were the interactions of the drug-issue agendas of the presidents' public relations agendas, the media, and the public while controlling for the policy agenda and a real-world measure of the severity of the drug problem? Finally, how did the relationships of these agendas differ during the Reagan and Bush presidencies?

A descriptive analysis of the media content indicates that the media's picture of the drug issue was cyclic and structured by drug issues and events, both real and politically contrived. The *preproblem* stage (July 1984–May 1986) was structured by drug-related events of sports heroes, the arrest of John deLorean, the death of DEA agent Enrique Camarena Salazar, and the political issue of President Reagan's drug-testing policy. In the *discovery* stage (June 1986–December 1987), media coverage was structured by the events of Len Bias' death and the political issues of Reagan's war on drugs, which focused on the political issues of testing, military use, and visible internal and external administrative actions. In the *plateau* stage (January 1988–January 1990), media coverage was structured around the very real-world issue of drug-related violence and crime and the very politically driven events of Colombia, Manuel Noriega, and President Bush's plan, war, and drug czar. Finally, in the *decline* stage (February 1990-June 1991), the media's coverage was structured by drug-related violence and crime and the political events surrounding Mayor Barry, the drug lords of Colombia, the indictment of Manuel Noriega, and the transition of power in the drug czar's office. The media content indicated a tone of success for the government's efforts, but objective measures indicated that the drug problems continued.

A descriptive analysis of the content of presidential public relations activities indicated that the presidents' efforts were also cyclic; however, unlike the media, they were structured more heavily by an emphasis on issues concerning the drug problem as opposed to specific drug-related events. The preproblem stage was structured by the drug-related issues of education/prevention, U.S. administration, international administration, military use, and U.S. enforcement. Although the media focused heavily on sports, testing, Salazar, and deLorean during the pre-problem stage, the president's major thrust of education/prevention seemed to relate more closely to Nancy Reagan's antidrug education crusade.

In the discovery stage, presidential public relations activities were structured by the issues of U.S. administration, education/prevention, testing, international administration, and demand. The president's priorities during this stage roughly matched the media's issue agenda of testing, U.S. administration, and international administration, although not in that order. The media tended to highlight the issue of testing much more heavily, and focused on the use of the military and on Len Bias' death, which the president only addressed as a secondary focus in his efforts.

In the plateau stage, presidential public relations activities were structured by the issues of U.S. administration, education/prevention, international administration, violence, demand, funding, and AIDS. The presidential priorities during this stage roughly matched the media's agenda of violence, Noriega, Columbia, Bush's plan, Bush's war on drugs, and the drug czar; however, the media tended to focus more heavily on the event aspects of the drug issue whereas the presidents, to a degree, tended to deal with the drug problem in a broader, issue format.

Finally, in the decline stage, presidential public relations activities were structured by the issues of education/prevention, U.S. administration, political use of the drug issue, international administration, violence, and funding. As in the plateau stage, presidential priorities during the decline stage roughly matched the media's agenda of violence, Colombia, Noriega, and the drug czar, but again the media tended to focus more heavily on the event aspects of the drug issue, whereas the president tended to deal with the problem in a broader, issue format.

The analysis of the interactions of agendas over time, based on ARIMA modeling and Granger causality tests, indicates the effects of real-world cues and policy on public opinion, the effect of public opinion on the media agenda, and the effect of the media on presidential agenda—an agenda that followed rather than led. The study finally indicated differences in the relationships of the agendas in the time frames of the Reagan and Bush administrations; however, these differences were not due to differences in the presidents, but rather were the result of the mounting drug problem and the resulting media and public concern. Reagan and Bush's agendas were both driven by the media's agenda, although Bush appeared to react a little more quickly than Reagan.

ACKNOWLEDGMENTS

The author offers his deepest appreciation to the following individuals for their assistance in this project: My wife, Lisa, and daughter, Alexandra, for their patience and kindness; Dr. Maxwell McCombs, Dr. Jennings Bryant, and Hollis Heimbouch for their editorial guidance and expertise; Dr. Robert L. Stevenson for his research vision and friendship; Dr. Donald Shaw for his insights into agenda setting; Professor Philip Meyer for his significant contribution to the project's conceptualization; Dr. Gary D. Gaddy for his patience and assistance with data analysis; Dr. Charlotte Mason for her vision of research methods; Barbara Semonche, Sue Dodd, and David Sheaves for their assistance in data collection; and Lana Harrison, NIDA, Joseph Gfroerer, NIDA, and Peter Sutton, Cambridge Reports, for their assistance with the project.

William J. Gonzenbach

Introduction

"The drug problem illustrates how issues rise and fall almost capriciously on the agendas of news organizations, politicians and the public" (Barrett, 1990, p. 1). This was certainly the case of the drug issue from 1984 to 1991. Richard Nixon was incorrect in 1973; the United States had not turned the corner on drug addiction. The drug problem continued, in varying degrees, and caught the attention of the press, the president, and the public, in varying degrees, in the second half of the 1980s and early 1990s. A study of issue agendas in the United States indicates that drugs "have generally not been on the systemic agenda in this century, except for two periods: the late 1960s, and the late 1980s," and that "the second period corresponds to a much greater preoccupation with the problem than the first" (Baumgartner & Jones, 1993, p. 153).

The first major surge of national attention to drugs under President Reagan in the 1980s came with his emphasis on interdiction, enforcement, and punishment rather than education, and a similar tactic by President Bush followed his election in 1988. Others concurred with this view that the rise and fall of the issue relates to the concern and emphasis the president has given to the issue, as exemplified by the two presidents' wars on drugs (Barrett, 1990; Shannon, 1990). Others speculated that the issue was driven by the media: "Lacking any objective evidence of a drug epidemic, we must look to the media themselves to determine why the drug issue received such a concentrated amount of coverage in such a short time" (Kerr, 1986). Finally, others theorized that the public can only accommodate a limited number of agenda items, which, like billiard balls, can be knocked by the break of events from the table, and thus rely on the focus of the media, political leaders, and interest groups for their survival on the public agenda (Shaw & McCombs, 1989). This book examines the drug issue from mid-1984 to mid-1991 with a broadened conceptualization of agenda setting to determine how drug-related issues and events and the primary agendas drove the issue over time.

Agenda research has had two main research traditions since the 1980s: *agenda setting,* a process examined mostly by communication researchers through which the mass media communicate the relative salience of various events and issues to the public, and *agenda building,* a process examined primarily by political scientists and sociologists through which the policy agendas of political elites are influenced by a variety of factors, including media agendas and public agendas (Rogers & Dearing, 1988).

Rogers and Dearing's agenda-setting model (see Fig. 1) offers a broad conceptualization of the agenda process and incorporates three main components: media agenda setting, in which the main dependent variable is the media's news agenda; public agenda setting, in which the main dependent variable is the content and order of topics in the public agenda; and policy agenda setting, the distinctive aspect of which is its concern with policy as a response to both the media agenda and the public agenda. The model also comprises three other components: influence agents, such as gatekeepers, influential media, and spectacular news events; personal experience and interpersonal communication about the issue of concern; and real-world cues about the importance of an issue, which offer an objective measure of the severity of the issue devoid of the *fictions,* or the representations of the issue created by people (see Lippmann, 1922).

Agenda setting, a term used henceforth to refer to the entire agenda process, is by definition a time-related process, yet the seminal work of presidential voting in Chapel Hill, North Carolina (McCombs & Shaw, 1972), and many other investigations of the agenda-setting process were based on cross-sectional data analyses that could not capture the essence of time in the agenda-setting process (Rogers & Dearing, 1988). Agenda setting often has been approached as a nonprocess because it has been generally treated as one part of the general quest by mass-communication scholars for media effects.

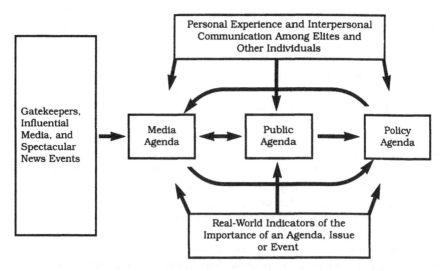

FIG. 1. Rogers and Dearing's (1988) agenda-setting model. Reprinted by permission of Sage Publications, Inc.

Another methodological approach, though rare, that developed at the same time as the early cross-sectional studies was trend analysis, which used longitudinal data to examine the trend in opinion and its relationship to the media over long periods of time (Brosius & Kepplinger, 1990a; e.g., Funkhouser, 1973). These studies were methodologically weak in that they tended to rely on an "eyeballing" of the data, yet offered the foundation for the examination of agenda setting as a time-related process. Later studies of the agenda-setting process employed panel designs with cross-lagged correlation analysis (e.g., Shaw & McCombs, 1977; Sohn, 1978; Tipton, Haney, & Basehart, 1975), but these studies failed to address many of the important mathematical properties of a time-related process, such as stationarity and autocorrelation (Kessler & Greenberg, 1981), and only focused on the agenda-setting process at a few points in time.

Stationarity means a time series has no secular trend, or that there is no systematic increase or decrease in the level of the series as it drifts upwards or downwards over time. Most of the time series encountered in the social sciences do have secular trend and therefore are *non*stationary. *Autocorrelation* means that observations of one variable from different points in time are correlated, or some observation Y_t (an observation in a series at some point in time) is predicted by a previous observation in the series Y_{t-1}. These concepts are covered in much greater detail later in this volume; however, these definitions should provide the necessary basis to understand the concepts.

In the late 1970s, researchers began to use time-series analysis that incorporated regression methods, some of which addressed the important mathematical properties of a time-related process such as autocorrelation within the series, to examine the relationships of agendas over time (e.g., Behr & Iyengar, 1985; Watt & van den Berg, 1978, 1981; Winter & Eyal, 1981). However, these methodological approaches did not fully model the mathematical time-related components of the time series, thus offering findings that may have been confounded by autocorrelated time processes (McCleary & Hay, 1980).

Finally, agenda-setting research turned to ARIMA (Autoregressive, Integrated, Moving Average) modeling to address the numerous problems and issues of autocorrelation in time-series analysis (e.g., Dearing, 1989; Gonzenbach, 1992; Rogers, Dearing, & Chang, 1991). In one of these few ARIMA studies, Rogers et al. asked how this agenda-setting process works over time and stated that a broader conceptualization of agenda-setting research that "considers influences among various agendas while focusing on issue competition, the role of new information about an issue, and changing media interpretations is likely to be more useful in explaining the development of an issue through the agenda-setting process" (p. 7). The study expanded on Dearing's (1989) study of the agenda-setting effects of the polling agenda about AIDS and analyzed the AIDS issue in the 1980s using 91 consecutive monthly time intervals to illustrate what they called a broadened agenda-setting perspective. The study explains how a social issue could remain on the national agenda for years because of the "interplay of a) constantly new information about the issue, which, when interpreted by journalists and editors in the context of the ongoing social problem, remakes the issue as being important in a new way, and b) attention given to the issue on agendas other than the mass-media agenda, such as the scientific agenda, the polling agenda, the public agenda, and the policy agenda" (Rogers et al., 1991, p. 2). The study provided a unique examination of how new information and media interpretations kept the issue alive in the 1980s and the study's methodology modeled the time series with ARIMA modeling, thus addressing key methodological concerns about stationarity and autocorrelation that previous agenda-setting research had failed to consider.

Although the work of Rogers et al. (1991) provides a new methodological direction for agenda-setting research, their study and previous agenda-setting research possess two limitations that need to be addressed. First, the study did not include a measure of public opinion about the AIDS issue; rather, the authors substituted a measure comprising the number of poll questions asked about AIDS over time as a surrogate for the public agenda. Although they concluded that the mass media set the public agenda for AIDS, they never directly tested the relationship of media salience and public salience. This poses a major limitation in the analysis of the Rogers and Dearing (1988) model.

Second, Rogers et al. (1991) included a science agenda as a measure of an influential media. This measure was operationalized as the number of articles about AIDS published in four leading medical and science journals. Although the measure seems appropriate for their AIDS study, this study of the drug issue in particular and future agenda-setting process research in general should consider the role of public relations as a driving force (or gatekeeper) in the agenda-setting process. At an empirical level, analyses of the influence of public relations on news content and on the public suggest that public relations deserves significant consideration as a crucial element of the agenda-setting process (Cutlip, 1962; Lippmann, 1922; Turk, 1985, 1986a, 1986b), especially in terms of presidential public-relations efforts for prominent national issues such as the drug issue. As Behr and Iyenger (1985) concluded, "When the president speaks, the public listens" (p. 54).

This analysis of the drug issue from mid-1984 to mid-1991 builds on Rogers et al.'s (1991) recommendation to examine other issues with their broaden conceptualization of agenda setting and proposes to address the aforementioned limitations of prior research. The analysis of the drug issue is framed around four primary research questions about the agenda-setting process. First, how did the media structure the interpretations and presentations of issue and event information during this period? This question is addressed with a detailed content analysis of the drug issue. Second, how did the president structure the interpretations and presentations of issue and event information during this period? This question is addressed with a detailed content analysis of presidential public relations activities. Third, what were the interactions of the drug-issue agendas of the presidents' public relations agendas, the media, and the public, while controlling for the policy agenda and a real-world measure of the severity of the drug problem? Fourth, how did the relationships of these agendas differ during the Reagan and Bush presidencies? The study's third and fourth research questions are addressed with ARIMA time-series analyses that examine and unravel the rather intertwined relationships of these agendas over time.

This book is comprised of seven chapters. Chapter 1, The Drug Issue: Its History, Events, and Issue Type, presents the history of the drug issue from mid-1984 to mid-1991 and attempts to qualitatively capture the cyclic pattern of agendas concerning the drug issue during this period. The chapter also examines theoretical investigations to determine the media's treatment of the drug issue and which theoretical model is best suited to examine this issue over time. The chapter also defines and examines the relationship between an issue and the events that form the issue, and a topology of issues is examined to help categorize the drug issue and the possible agenda-setting ramifications of this categorization.

Chapter 2, Measuring Agendas and Agenda Relationships Over Time, presents a review and analysis of the methods used by agenda-setting researchers to measure agendas and agenda relationships. The examination begins with cross-sectional approaches and progresses to time-based approaches such as trend studies, panel, and time-series designs. Finally, a fairly detailed analysis of ARIMA modeling and time-series designs is presented. Chapter 3, Conceptual Considerations and Measures, presents the research questions and specific hypotheses, the methodological approaches for the content analyses and time-series analyses, and the operationalization of the study's five agenda variables. Chapter 4, The Media's Structuring of the Drug Issue, examines the media's representation of the drug issue from mid-1984 to mid-1991 and presents the results of a content analysis of 10,062 news stories from *The New York Times* and the evening news broadcasts of ABC, NBC, and CBS. The chapter also examines the issue and event categories of the drug issue, and the cycle of this content over time. Finally, the relationship between the cycle of coverage and the media content is assessed.

Chapter 5, Presidential Public Relations, Federal Expenditures, Real-World Cues, and Public Opinion, primarily examines presidential public relations activities concerning the drug issue from mid-1984 to mid-1991. The chapter presents the results of a content analysis of 476 reports of presidential public relations activities from the Public Papers of the Presidents and also examines these activities in terms of the issue and event categories of the drug issue, and the cycle of this content over time. In addition, the relationship between the cycle of these activities and their issue content is assessed. Finally, the chapter examines the trend in total federal expenditures on the drug issue, the frequency of emergency-room admissions for cocaine (the real-world cue measure), and public opinion about drugs as the most important problem facing the country.

Chapter 6, ARIMA Modeling and Analysis of the Drug Issue Agendas, examines the univariate analyses of each of the five agenda time series. The results of the Granger causality tests for each permutation of the five agendas is then examined, and the multivariate analyses and models are presented. The chapter concludes with a comparison of the relationship of agendas within the Reagan and Bush presidencies. Chapter 7, The Drug Issue, 1984-1991: Conclusions and Implications, then assesses the findings and implications of the study and charts recommendations for future time-series based, agenda-setting research.

Chapter 1

The Drug Issue: Its History, Events, and Issue Type

The road to determine how the media and president have structured interpretations and presentations of drug issue and event information over time and the relationships of the primary drug-issue agendas over time needs to begin by addressing some basic questions. First, what are the key historical pieces that comprised the drug issue from mid-1984 to mid-1991? Second, what do theoretical investigations tell us about the media's treatment of the drug issue and which theoretical model is best suited to examine this issue over time? Third, how are issues and events defined and measured in agenda setting? Fourth, are there different categorizations of issue types that will theoretically lead to differences in agenda-setting effects? This chapter addresses these four questions as a prelude to this book's primary objectives.

THE HISTORY OF THE DRUG ISSUE: 1984–1991

Survey data from the Institute for Social Research at the University of Michigan indicate that drug usage actually decreased in 1981; however, the large-scale introduction of crack cocaine in 1985, with its increased purity and low price, led to an increased concern and fear (Johnston, 1989). As an example, total emergency-room mentions of cocaine from the National Institute of Drug Abuse's Warning Network (DAWN) rose dramatically in the second half of the 1980s (Adams, Blanken, Ferguson, & Kopstein, 1990). Given the impact of crack cocaine, it may be fair to say that the United States did have a drug crisis beginning in 1985, if one accounts for the addictive potential of cocaine, the increasingly dangerous form of crack cocaine, the rapidly increasing rate of casualties, the increased availability and decreasing price of cocaine, and the degree of penetration of cocaine use into the younger population. As Johnston (1989) concluded, "It was admittedly a qualitatively different drug crisis than the one that existed in 1980...marijuana use had especially declined, and use of amphetamines and barbiturates was also down—but more people were at risk of addiction and overdose reactions because of what they were using and how they were using it" (p. 109).

The government had begun to address the drug issue long before the advent of crack cocaine in 1985. National Institute on Drug Abuse (NIDA) research from the 1970s and early 1980s indicated that public awareness of the dangers of drug abuse was very low. In 1982, NIDA began to design the "Just Say No" campaign, the objective being to present a drug-free life as the healthy norm for teenagers (Lachter & Forman, 1989). The campaign was formally organized in 1984 and launched in 1985, with the help of Nancy Reagan. The "Just Say No" campaign helped her emerge from a rough start in the White House. By January 1985, she had made 14 antidrug speeches and made appearances supporting the "Just Say No" campaign on PBS' "The Chemical People," ABC's "Good Morning America," and the family-targeted situation comedy "Diff'rent Strokes" (After a Rough,1985).

Although NIDA and Nancy Reagan focused their attention on the youth of America beginning in 1984, the media's major focus concerning drugs was on the drug-related escapades of auto maker John deLorean, who attempted and failed to use a large drug deal to save his failing car company. As an example, *The New York Times* and the national television networks featured 16 stories in July and 42 in August of 1984 about deLorean.

In February 1985, President Reagan focused part of his State of the Union speech on the drug issue. In line with his minimized government involvement theme, he focused on the elements of care and treatment of addicts by concerned volunteers; however, directly after the speech, U. S. Drug Enforcement Agent Enrique Camarena Salazar was kidnapped and killed by drug lords in Mexico. The event helped aim the spotlight of the media. The networks and *The New York Times* featured 88 stories on the event during February, March, and April of 1985, and the event focused President Reagan's attention on relations with Mexico concerning drug importation. In mid-1985, the media's eye was also drawn to the use of drugs by celebrities, as baseball stars Denny McLain and Joe Pepitone faced drug arrests and British authorities arrested actor Stacy Keach for possession of a controlled substance. Organized crime also entered the media's spotlight in September 1985 as authorities in New York cracked the "pizza connection," a $1.6 billion heroin ring concealed in New York pizzerias. However, a conversation between political activist Jesse Jackson and A. M. Rosenthal, executive director of *The New York Times,* in the fall of 1985 may have been the most important drug-related event of the drug-issues history in the 1980s. Jackson met with Rosenthal to discuss the devastating, destructive forces of drugs, especially cocaine and crack cocaine, on the minority community. Subsequently, *The Times* assigned a reporter to cover drug-related stories full time and, on November 29, 1985, published its first front-page story on crack, a new form of inexpensive cocaine just beginning to enter the United States (Kerr, 1986; McCombs, Einsiedel, & Weaver, 1991).

The Times' leadership role and this article set off a barrage of coverage of the drug issue beginning with a *Newsweek* cover story in March 1986, features by *The Times* in April about the wide-spread sale of crack, and simultaneous publication on May 18, 1986, of features about drugs in all three of New York City's major newspapers (McCombs et al., 1991). The newspaper coverage also set the agenda for television, which capped the "'grand finale' in this 6-month barrage of drug coverage during 1986" (p. 44) with specials about cocaine on both NBC and CBS in September, including a CBS documentary entitled "48 Hours on Crack Street," which aired on September 2, and NBC's "Cocaine Country," which aired on September 5. On September 23, PBS' "McNeil/Lehrer News Hour" also featured a 22-minute segment on whether the drug problem was hyped by the media (Reese & Danielian, 1989).

The media coverage of the issue in 1986 was also driven by several political and nonpolitical events. To counter increasing cocaine use among older teenagers and young adults, NIDA developed a multimedia program called "Cocaine, The Big Lie," which was implemented in two phases, the first in April 1986 and the second in Spring 1988. Needham Harper Worldwide produced 13 public service announcements for the first phase, which aired 1,500 to 2,500 times per month within 75 local television markets, according to the Broadcast Advertisers Report, Inc. (Lachter & Forman, 1989). The second phase of "The Big Lie" program, which began in Spring 1988, targeted messages to high school and college students as well as to families and friends of users.

In early 1986 President Reagan began to focus on the issue of drug testing for government employees, which culminated in 124 stories in *The Times* and network news between July and September of 1986. This testing focus was also picked up by the business community, as exemplified by the 30 stories in *The Times* and network news about corporate drug testing in March 1986.

A major drug story of 1986 was the death of Len Bias, a basketball star from the University of Maryland, who died from a crack cocaine overdose in June of that year. The tragedy captured the attention of *The Times* and the networks, which presented 62 stories about Bias in June and July. Bias' death, combined with the spread of crack cocaine and President Reagan's war on drugs, which began in August 1986, heightened the attention on the issue, culminating in Congressional passage of the $1.7 billion Omnibus Drug Bill in December 1986.

In his war on drugs, Reagan turned to the use of the military to combat the importation of drugs, as exemplified by the nearly 60 stories about the use of the military to stop drugs presented by *The Times* and the networks between July and October of 1986 and an increased focus on the use of U.S. drug enforcement agencies to assist this effort. The events of the summer of 1986 also focused the media's attention on public opinion about the drug issue, as suggested by the 14 stories in September by *The Times* and networks about public opinion concerning the drug issue. The percentage of American adults considering drugs to be "the most important problem facing the country" rose from 1–3% to about 10–15% during this time (see Fig. 5.12).

The escalation of attention by the media and President Reagan faded in 1987, and *The Times* suggested in March 1987 that Reagan's war had "fizzled." Conversely, President Reagan claimed, "The tide of the battle has turned, and we are beginning to win the crusade for a drug-free America" (Lichter & Lichter, 1989, p. 2).

Barrett (1990) argued that, as in 1984, the drug issue did not play a major role in the presidential election of 1988. As an example, *The Times* and networks carried only 64 stories in 1988 specifically concerning the drug issue and the presidential election. However, a study from the Center for Media and Public Affairs that examined media coverage of drugs from January 25 through October 31, 1988, indicated (as does this study's data) a sharp increase in coverage of the issue in the spring of 1988 (Lichter & Lichter, 1989). Lichter and Lichter suggested that during this time drug abuse became the subject of an ongoing policy debate in Washington, as an election debate waged throughout the country. In addition, public concern increased due to international disputes with Latin American nations like Panama, Mexico, and Colombia. In the spring of 1988, Reagan continued his rhetoric about enforcement, the use of the military, and international relations concerning drugs. During this time, the second phase of "Cocaine: The Big Lie" program took place, with public service messages being targeted to high-school and college students, as well as to families and friends of users.

In early 1988 the media spotlight also began to focus on the relationship between intravenous drug use and AIDS and the emerging voices of citizen groups protesting about the problems associated with drugs, as indicated by 37 articles in 1988 by *The Times* and the networks about these unofficial "voices" concerned about the drug problem. News about drugs in 1988 was preeminently news about cocaine; marijuana and hashish provided a strong secondary focus, especially after the Reagan administration's zero-tolerance policy cast greater attention on recreational users. Drug users portrayed on the television news tended to be poor, inner-city Blacks addicted to crack cocaine or heroin and middle- or upper-class suburban White users of cocaine or marijuana. The debate over drugs was one of the top 10 topics covered on TV news during 1988, even after excluding reports that treated drugs in the context of other major stories, such as the election, Panama, and crime news (Lichter & Lichter, 1989).

After George Bush was elected president in November 1988, polls showed drugs were a major concern of the public during the first few months of his administration in 1989, with about 20–25% of American adults citing drugs as "the most important issue facing the country." Congress had passed a law to establish an office to coordinate and intensify the federal drug effort. President Bush developed his war on drugs, especially in terms of the supply of drugs from Colombia, and appointed William Bennett, the former secretary of education, to head the Office of National

Drug Control Policy. Although drug use actually decreased and leveled off in 1988 (Adams et al., 1990), Bennett immediately urged the President Bush to make drugs America's "Number 1" priority and coaxed the President to address the American public about the seriousness of the problem on television (Barrett, 1990). Bush addressed the American public—with a bag of crack cocaine in hand—on September 5, 1989. The speech stirred both media interest and public attention. Public opinion polls after the speech indicated that almost two thirds of the American public considered drugs to be the country's most important problem ("The Other War," 1990). Television coverage of the issue increased from 2 to 12 drug stories per night; however, the media intensity began to diminish and within a month the networks were again averaging about 2 stories per night. The television coverage after President Bush's television appearance on September 29 through June 1990 continued to have a heavy portrayal of Blacks using drugs. Only 32% of the drug-related visuals on television showed only Whites and 50% of the visuals showed only non-Whites, most of whom were Black (Lichter & Lichter, 1990).

In early 1990, federal surveys indicated that the casual consumption of drugs was down, as were emergency-room admissions and death rates from drug overdoses (Shannon, 1990). Drugs as a media event seemed to lose their appeal, as indicated by Fox Television's decision to drop a special presentation, "City Under Siege," in April 1990. Public consideration of drugs to be the country's most important problem fell from a high of 66% in September 1988 to 25% in July 1990 (Barrett, 1990) and to around 10% in October 1990 ("The Other War," 1990). The attention of the press, the president, and the public shifted to matters of economics and the Persian Gulf (Shannon, 1990). Many considered the problem to be a matter of poor, inner-city, Black residents. This "ghettoization" of the problem shifted its importance for the White majority, who no longer saw the problem to be dramatic or devastating (Barrett, 1990). In light of the serious problems of recession, taxes, and the Persian Gulf, the drug issue also seemed to become a difficult, no-win issue for President Bush, and thus he preferred to announce that "we are on the road to victory" and focus his attention elsewhere. Others speculated that the media were doing the same.

THE DRUG ISSUE AND AGENDA INFLUENCES OVER TIME

The rise and fall of the drug issue on the American agenda from 1984 to 1991 may not be as capricious as Barrett (1990) speculated. The history of the drug issue indicates that attention to it from mid-1984 to mid-1991 may have comprised a tangled web driven by information campaigns, the media agenda, the presidents' public-relations agendas and the public's perception of the issue. Sociological theory suggests that media and other elements of the community social system mutually influence each other over time regarding social issues and problems (K.

A. Smith, 1987). Therefore, key issues to address are what theoretical investigations tell us about the media's treatment of the drug issue and which theoretical model is best suited to examine this issue over time.

Recent studies about the drug issue suggest patterns in media coverage over time that may be correlated to the trends in public opinion. A study of national media coverage of the drug issue between 1983 and 1987 indicated "a classic pattern: There was a slow initial increase in overall media attention, followed by a shift in emphasis to subject matters of broader interest. Then, interest in drugs increased sharply, peaked, and declined." The emergence of the drug issue differed from other issues "because the national issue was subjected to strong public information campaigns from the National Institute on Drug Abuse and was exploited to some extent by politicians in 1986 as national elections approached" (Merriam, 1989, p. 21). These influences were accentuated by other events, most specifically the death of Len Bias in June 1986. "Bias' death posed an almost media-perfect example of the dangers of drug overdose.... Concern for his death matched closely with the concerns national media and government leaders were seeking to present" (p. 21). The issue declined after Bias' death and President Reagan's war on drugs (August–October, 1986). The impetus for a reemergence of the issue could have come from the arrival of new drug types or from increased emphasis on drugs from national leaders, both of which did occur (Merriam, 1989).

This change in media emphasis for an issue and its relationship to public attention over time has been examined by several researchers. The natural-history model suggests that social problems progress through historical stages in time once they have been defined as a public issue through mass-media coverage (Downs, 1972). The public-arena model examines the competition among many social problems and their elements as they compete for newspaper column inches and broadcast time (Hilgartner & Bosk, 1988). This model, like the natural-history model, has trouble accounting for issues that remain on the media's agenda for long periods of time (Rogers et al., 1991). The *ecology of news perspective* suggests that certain public issues will persist in mass media coverage over relatively long periods of time through the interplay of journalistic and nonjournalistic actors (Molotch, Protess, & Gordon, 1987); however, the researchers did not demonstrate this with cases of prolonged mass-media coverage of public issues (Rogers et al., 1991). The agenda-setting model provides the best way to examine the relationships of agendas concerning an issue and the pattern of an issue over time because it subsumes both natural-history models and public-arena models of public-issue development and relies on both the idea of cyclical change in attention to issues and the idea of competition between issues as a determinant of change.

THE ROLE OF EVENTS IN THE LIFE OF AN ISSUE

Another primary question that must be addressed in any agenda-setting study is "What is an issue?" Agenda-setting research has studied a wide range of issues, but little care has been given to defining exactly what an issue is (Rogers & Dearing, 1988). An important way to conceptualize an issue is by distinguishing issues from events. An *event* is defined as discrete happenings that are limited by space and time, and an *issue* is defined as involving cumulative news coverage of a series of related events that fit together in a broad category (Shaw, 1977). Rogers and Dearing (1988) concluded that "events are specific components of issues" (p. 566). As an example, the drug-related death in 1986 of college athlete Len Bias was a news event that helped put the drug issue on the national agenda, even though total drug use in the American public was declining during the period.

This distinction between issues and events is the foundation for determining how new information affects the restructuring of the media's agenda over time. If journalists do not have new information about an issue, news coverage will stop. This new information, or *event information* as it is referred to in this book, is necessary for news gatekeepers to consider an "old" issue newsworthy, and the new information must allow journalists to restructure the issue in a new light. When the frequency of monthly media coverage of an issue is plotted over time, the plot is usually a recurring (and sometimes exponential in growth) cycle, with each cycle, or portion of the cycle, representing a restructuring of the issue via event information: "The over-time content of the media coverage of an issue represents not only new information, but also periodic changes in how journalists, editors, and hence viewers and readers, interpret the old issue in light of new information" (Rogers et al., 1991, pp. 3–4).

A study of the AIDS issue from 1981 to 1988 divided the 91 months of the study period into four eras: *Initial* (June 1981–April 1983); *Science* (May 1983–June 1985); *Human* (July 1985–January 1987); and *Political* (February 1987–December 1988). These eras were statistically determined with tests that determined the significance of differences in the cycles of media coverage of the issue for the 91 monthly intervals. A content analysis of the subissues of AIDS was then used to determine the focus of each of the eras and the frequencies of each of the subissue categories over the 91-month period. The content analysis comprised the following media: *The New York Times*, the *Washington Post*, the *Los Angeles Times*, and the network evening newscasts of ABC, CBS, and NBC. The initial era represented a period of minimal media attention to the AIDS issue; the science era depended heavily on new scientific information about AIDS; the human era was characterized by the personalization of the AIDS issue by heavy media coverage of the Rock Hudson and Ryan White news events; and the political era focused on a variety of public controversies, especially public policy about AIDS concerning mandatory testing and individual privacy (Rogers et al., 1991).

AGENDA SETTING AND ISSUE TYPES

A final preliminary question to examine in agenda-setting research is whether there are different categorizations of issue types that theoretically lead to differences in agenda-setting effects. Agenda-setting effects are conditional on the nature of the issue being studied. Researchers have offered several ways to categorize issues. Unidirectional causality (i.e., media salience leads to public salience) should occur for *unobtrusive issues,* which include the issues of drug abuse and pollution, in which events create issues with which people ordinarily have no direct experience (Zucker, 1978). An individual tends to rely on the mass media for information and an interpretation of the issue when the individual has had less direct experience with the issue. Conversely, for *obtrusive issues*—issues with which individuals had greater familiarity such as cost of living and unemployment—salience in the public agenda leads to salience in the media agenda. These results were confirmed by a factor analysis that categorized agenda items as being obtrusive and unobtrusive, as being opposed judgmental determinations (Eyal, 1979; Rogers & Dearing, 1988). One of the major revisions in agenda-setting research is whether different types of issues may be characterized by unique agenda-setting dynamics over time, most specifically obtrusive and unobtrusive issues (Neuman, 1990; Neuman, Just, & Crigler, 1988; Zucker, 1978). In regard to issue differences, Neuman (1990) offered a topology of issues. One element of the topology, *symbolic crises,* examines the role of unobtrusive issues, exemplified by the drug issue, in which "a combination of events and the responses of the government, the public and the media leads to a public definition of the issue as a problem of crisis proportions for a limited period of time" (p. 169).

We may also categorize as either *concrete* or *abstract* (Yagade & Dozier, 1990). "Whereas obtrusiveness of an issue is the degree to which an issue forces itself into the direct experiences of individuals, the abstractness of an issue is the degree to which an issue is difficult to conceptualize, to be made sensible" (p. 4). Abstract issues reduce agenda-setting effects because individuals find it difficult to attach salience to something they do not comprehend, whereas concrete issues enhance agenda-setting effects. For the drug issue, which was categorized as a concrete issue, media salience increases public salience.

This study of the drug issue operates on the assumption that the drug issue is an unobtrusive, concrete issue that can be categorized as a symbolic crisis in which a combination of events and the responses of the government, the public, and the media lead to a public definition of the issue as a problem of crisis proportions for a limited period of time. Research suggests that the media agenda will have a unidirectional effect on the public agenda for this unobtrusive, concrete issue.

CONCLUSION

The qualitative analysis of the history of the drug issue from mid-1984 to mid-1991 suggests that the issue comprises a tangled array of dramatic events, information campaigns, presidential public relations, and cyclic patterns of media and public interest.

An analysis of relevant research suggested the following: First, agenda setting provides the best model to examine the relationships of agendas concerning an issue and the pattern of an issue over time because it relies on both the idea of cyclical change in attention to issues and the idea of competition between issues as a determinant of change. Second, at least from 1983 to 1987, media coverage of the drug issue indicated a classic pattern of attention: There was a slow initial increase in overall media attention, followed by a shift in emphasis to subject matters of broader interest, and then interest in drugs increased sharply, peaked, and declined. The impetus for a reemergence of the issue could come from the arrival of new drug types or from increased emphasis on drugs from national leaders, both of which did occur.

Third, an *event* is defined as discrete happenings that are limited by space and time, and an *issue* is defined as involving cumulative news coverage of a series of related events that fit together in a broad category; that is, events are specific components of issues. Also, this distinction between issues and events is the foundation for an answer to how new information affects the restructuring of the media's agenda over time. This new information, or event information, is necessary for news gatekeepers to consider an "old" issue newsworthy, and the new information must allow journalists to restructure the issue in a new light. When the frequency of monthly media coverage of an issue is plotted over time, the plot is usually a recurring (and sometimes exponential in growth) cycle, with each cycle, or portion of the cycle, representing a restructuring of the issue via event information.

Fourth, different types of issues do indeed have unique agenda-setting effects and fifth, the drug issue is defined as an unobtrusive, concrete issue that can be categorized as a symbolic crisis in which a combination of events and the responses of the government, the public, and the media lead to a public definition of the issue as a problem of crisis proportions for a limited period of time. Finally, the media agenda will have a unidirectional, or one-way, effect on the public agenda for this unobtrusive, concrete issue.

Chapter 2

Measuring Agendas and Agenda Relationships Over Time

Studies concerning the relationships among agenda setting's primary variables present a rather confusing picture. The inconsistency of the results is certainly due in part to the agenda-setting effects of specific issue types. However, Iyengar and Kinder (1987; cited in Rogers & Dearing, 1988) offered much more serious and biting reasons for the inconsistency of results:

> Although research on agenda-setting has proliferated over the past decade, so far, the results add up to rather little. With a few important exceptions, agenda-setting research has been theoretically naive, methodologically primitive, both confused and confusing.... Agenda-setting may be an apt metaphor, but it is no theory. (p. 557)

As a foundation for the analysis of examining the relationships among the drug-issue agendas, this chapter specifically examines the major methodological approaches used to examine agendas and agenda-setting relationships over time. Iyengar and Kinder's (1987) conclusion about agenda-setting methodologies may be correct, but this study takes issue with the spirit of the statement. Agenda-setting process research presents many methodological problems concerning the measurement of agendas and agenda relationships over time; however, the body of research indicates that the methodological approaches have grown with the emerging time-series databases and methodological techniques and have built on the earnest efforts and visions of the field's fledgling analyses.

Although agenda setting is by definition a time-related process, many of the early agenda-setting studies were based on cross-sectional data, which by definition cannot directly capture the relationships of the agendas over time (Rogers & Dearing, 1988; Weaver, 1987). A social process may go through various phases, rising and falling with the influence of various agendas and their operatives' efforts to frame and energize the issue for the public, who may in turn effect the life of an issue via their public outcries. The effects that one measures will certainly depend on where in time and space one happens to examine the process of a specific issue. A cross-sectional study's static design cannot account fully for the dynamic nature of the agenda-setting process (Behr & Iyengar, 1985), nor can it account at all for time lags of possible effects (Brosius & Kepplinger, 1990a).

Early agenda-setting research focused too narrowly on short time frames because the researchers came from an effects tradition, but the methodological progression in agenda-setting research has moved from "one-shot, cross-sectional studies to more sophisticated research designs that allow more precise exploration of agenda-setting as a process" (Rogers & Dearing, 1988, p. 572). This methodological progression can be categorized into four relevant methodological arenas: cross-sectional studies, trend studies, panel designs, and time-series designs (see Kessler & Greenberg, 1981).

CROSS-SECTIONAL STUDIES

Change effects in cross-sectional studies are inferred from variations between units at a single point in time. Although valuable insights can often be gleaned from this method, the approach is seriously flawed because it only measures synchronous relationships (relationships at the same point in time) and therefore cannot directly address time-based causality (Kessler & Greenberg, 1981). This approach should be avoided if possible whenever cohort or historical effects are presumed, at least when the focus of the research centers on change. In agenda-setting research, this approach is exemplified by the seminal research on agenda setting, in which media salience and public salience were correlated at one point in time (see McCombs & Shaw, 1972). Other studies used cross-sectional analyses to investigate the intervening role of individual-difference variables (e.g., Weaver, 1980) and other studies lagged media measures prior to a one-shot survey to examine the intervening roles of social category and social relationship variables (e.g., McLeod, Becker, & Byrnes, 1974) and to document time lags (Stone & McCombs, 1981).

TREND STUDIES

When a researcher is content with simply determining how much a single variable has changed in a population, he or she can gather measures from successive samples from the same population at different points in time and examine the change in the variable over time (Kessler & Greenberg, 1981). This type of study is referred to as a *trend study*. In agenda-setting research, the trend analysis' key weakness is that researchers have generally "eyeballed" the trend over time with rather simple graphic representations or applied analytic methods that do not adequately address the often complex mathematical nature of the time-series processes (Brosius & Kepplinger, 1990a; McCleary & Hay, 1980). However, these early studies made an important contribution to agenda-setting research in that they sought to examine the agenda-setting process over long periods of time and to disentangle the complexities of relationships of issue agendas over time.

The seminal trend analysis in agenda setting explored the dynamics of public opinion for eight issues from 1964 to 1970 (Funkhouser, 1973). The study examined, in chronological order, annual measures of the country's "most important problem" question from national surveys and then expanded on the basic trend approach by "eyeballing" the trend in opinion for these eight issues in relation to the annual number of articles that appeared in three national news magazines about each issue and to rather vague measures of real-world cues. In regard to the drug issue, media coverage roughly paralleled the rise in the real-world cue of actual drug use. However, the only evidence offered for the real-world cue was that "LSD was first noted in 1963, and from that point the use of that and other hallucinogenics (especially marijuana) accelerated through 1970" (p. 71). No statement was made about the relationship of media coverage and public opinion about drugs because no one considered drugs to be the country's most important problem until 1970, when 3% of those surveyed said it was.

In a similar vein, another analysis "eyeballed" the trend in opinion regarding the abortion issue with annual data from 1972 to 1976 (Tedrow & Mahoney, 1979). Unlike Funkhouser's (1973) study, it did not examine the data in relation to the media and real-world cue agendas; rather, it examined change in opinion in regard to gender, education, occupation, religion, and church attendance.

Beniger's (1978) study argued that media emphasis could be used as a surrogate measure for public salience and included a measure based on the Greenfield Index computed from the number of stories about an issue indexed in the *Reader's Guide to Periodical Literature*. The study examined annual measures of media coverage from 1945 to 1975 for numerous issues including drugs and "eyeballed" this media coverage in relation to real-world cues about accidental drug deaths (only 1966–1972), measures of self-reports of drug use (only from 1966), and the percentage of responses to drugs as the country's most important problem (only from 1969 to 1975). It concluded that media coverage may be more closely associated with public attitudes and opinion than are more objective measures.

Finally, a study by T. Smith (1980) examined the trend in opinion for numerous social issues from 1946 to 1976 based on the percentage of responses to "most important problem" questions from national surveys. The analysis "eyeballed" the trends in opinion over time and then, like Tedrow and Mahoney (1979), it examined these trends in opinion in relation to several demographic variables. However, d-systems, which are linear-flow graphs, were used to determine the differences for each of the demographic subgroups over time.

PANEL AND TIME-SERIES DESIGNS

Researchers use panel and time-series designs to examine the differences between units in patterns of change, or to determine the effects of a change in one variable on another variable. The investigation of such questions is aided by the collection of data at more than one point in time on the same units of analysis. The most commonly used design of this type is the time series, for which observations are collected on one person or other unit of analysis for a large number of time intervals (Kessler & Greenberg, 1981). The second method is the panel study, in which observations are collected for a number of individuals (or other units of analysis) instead of only one, at two or more points in time. In agenda-setting research, the major difference between the two is that in a panel study the unit of analysis is the individual, who is typically surveyed at only a few points in time; in a time-series analysis, the unit of analysis is typically an aggregate measure, such as the frequency of news stories, the percentage of the population believing an issue is the country's most important problem, or a real-world cue measure such as the unemployment rate. The typical time-series study usually includes numerous time points. In this analysis, two types of time-series analyses are examined separately: The first type uses correlation and regression methods to examine the time-series process; the second type uses ARIMA models to mathematically model the various time-series components (McCleary & Hay, 1980).

Panel Designs

Panel designs are powerful methods to provide information about cross-sectional and longitudinal variation (Kessler & Greenberg, 1981). In agenda-setting research, cross-lagged correlations are typically used to examine the relationship between two agendas. For example, a 1972 study of the national presidential election conducted in Charlotte, NC, compared the rank-order correlations of the media agenda of issues (both newspaper and television) and the public's agenda of issues (voter's agenda) from June 1972 to October 1972 (McCombs & Shaw, 1972). The study hypothesized that if Media (X_1) was a stronger cause of Public Opinion (Y_2) than Media (X_2) was of Public Opinion (Y_1), the correlation rX_1Y_2 should be larger in magnitude than the correlation rY_1X_2 (see Fig. 2.1).

This simple comparison presents several problems (Kessler & Greenberg, 1981; Markus, 1979; see Fig. 2.2). One type of problem involves temporal misspecification, or temporal erosion. If X and Y are measured at slightly different times, the misspecified causal lags can create significant observed cross-lagged correlation differences even when they do not exist in the true causal processes. Another class of problems concerns the consistency of effects across time, also called *stationarity*. If the reliability of one of the variables changes over time, or if the relationship between the measured variable and the underlying construct to which one is making some inference changes through time, the cross-lagged correlations will attenuate in ways unrelated to the relative causal influences. Finally, the cross-lagged

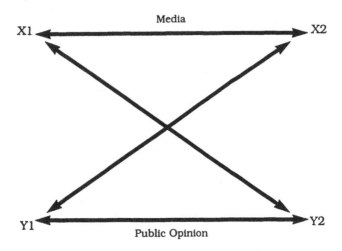

FIG. 2.1. Shaw and McComb's agenda-setting panel study model.

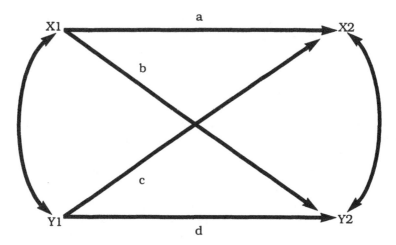

FIG. 2.2. Kessler and Greenberg's panel-study model.

correlation is inappropriate as a test of relative causal influence because lagged cross-correlations are determined not only by the differential stabilities of X to Y and from Y to X, but also by the differential stabilities of X to X and Y to Y.

The cross-lagged correlations can be expressed as follows from the fundamental theorem of path analysis:

$$rX_1Y_2 = b + drX_1Y_1$$
$$rY_1X_2 = c + arX_1Y_1.$$

The cross-lagged correlations receive contributions from the true causal coefficients b and c, but they also receive contributions proportional to the stabilities of a and d. Only when the stabilities of a and d are equal does equality of the causal coefficients b and c follow from equality of the cross-correlations. If a and d are not equal, no inference about the relative strength, or even sign, of the true causal inferences can be determined. If the purpose of one's analysis is to estimate causal parameters, then a multiple regression approach should be used in which the cross-lagged partial regression coefficients can be compared in a number of ways, or preferably, the correlation rX_2Y_2 can be decomposed into its component causal parts so that the relative influences of the cross-coefficients can be examined (Kessler & Greenberg, 1981).

Time-Series Designs

Like panel designs, time-series approaches are concerned with differences between units in a pattern of change, or in the effects of a change in one variable on another over time; however, unlike panel designs, the variables (at least in agenda-setting research) are typically aggregate measures collected over numerous points in time. Time-series designs in agenda-setting research build on the agenda-setting trend studies by charting agenda-setting measures over relatively long periods of time, but then use correlation and regression to empirically quantify the relationships of the measures over time.

The first such study examined the relationship between media coverage of an airport noise problem and public complaints to the Federal Aviation Administration's noise complaint telephone service over 253 consecutive days (Watt & van den Burg, 1978). The study is important because it addressed the issue of *autocorrelation,* which was defined as the "correlation of a variable with itself at different time intervals" (p. 219; also see Ostrom, 1990). Unfortunately, the study did not integrate the autocorrelation modeling into the cross-lagged correlation analysis (nor did it address the issue of stationarity) and thus the significance tests of the cross-lagged correlations may not be reliable (McCleary & Hay, 1980).

A study of civil rights used correlation methods to examine the relationship between public opinion and media coverage of the issue from 1954 to 1976 (Winter & Eyal, 1981). The public opinion measure comprised 27 measures of civil rights as the country's "most important problem" from national polls, gathered at unequal intervals, which were compared to a media measure comprising *The New York Times* front-page coverage of the issue that was collected for the 6 months preceding each poll. The study examined the correlation of the media agenda at monthly lags of 1 to 5 months to the public agenda. Although not presented under the guise of autocorrelation, the analysis partialed out prior monthly effects, which may have controlled for autocorrelation in the media series, whereas the study did not address autocorrelation in their "dependent" public opinion series, nor did it address the issue of stationarity.

A study by Behr and Iyengar (1985) provided an important contribution to time-series agenda-setting research by examining contrasting regression models that controlled for autocorrelation in the series to examine the relationships of television news coverage and public opinion, while controlling for real-world cue measures. In the study, which examined the obtrusive issues of energy, unemployment, and inflation, public opinion was measured by responses to "most important problem" questions for 42 consecutive bimonthly periods from 1974 to 1980. The analysis contrasted two regression equations for each issue:

TV News = c + Real World + Issue Importance + e
Issue Importance = C + TV News + Real World + E,
where c/C are constants and e/E are error terms.

The study moved beyond cross-lagged correlation approaches and addressed the issue of autocorrelation, though it does not address the issue of stationarity.

Another important study by Smith (1987) examined the relationships among the media agenda, public concerns, and public evaluations about local governmental services in Louisville with eight annual surveys conducted from 1974 to 1981. The study examined the relationships with a regression method based on the idea of Granger (1980) causality, a popular technique developed by an economist for estimating causality among variables measured from repeated cross-sectional surveys. "A variable is said to Granger cause Y, if Y can better be predicted from the past history (i.e., the lagged values) of X and Y together than the past history of Y alone. Sims (1972) has demonstrated that a necessary condition for a variable X to be considered exogenous (i.e., a causal predictor) to variable Y is that Y fails to Granger cause X. When X is found to Granger cause Y and Y Granger cause X, a two-way effect is indicated" (K. A. Smith,1987, p. 386).

Shoemaker, Wanta, and Leggett (1989) examined the media agenda and public opinion of the drug issue in the United States from 1972 to 1986 with a hierarchical regression approach that did not address the problems of autocorrelation or stationarity. The findings suggested that the more the media emphasized drugs, the more people thought drugs were the most important problem and that there was no evidence of similarity in coverage among the media; *The New York Times* and the *Los Angeles Times* accounted for almost all of the total effect of the nine media on public concern with drugs. The study also found evidence for media agenda-setting effects in two time periods—one during the weeks immediately preceding the poll and one about 3 months prior to the poll.

Kepplinger, Donsbach, Brosius, and Staab (1989) investigated the relationship between media coverage of German Chancellor Helmut Kohl in seven leading German print media and the opinions of the German public about the politician between 1975 and 1984. Cross-lagged correlations were used, which did not address autocorrelation or stationarity, to examine the relationship between media coverage and approval. They qualified the analysis by saying that ARIMA modeling or Granger causality was not used because of missing values and the less-than-optimal quality of the data. The study concluded the evaluation shifts in the media preceded similar evaluation shifts in public opinion with a time lag of about 3–6 months for the whole period of investigation, and a somewhat shorter time lag for the period of Kohl's chancellorship.

In 1990 several researchers made important contributions to time-series analysis in agenda setting by creating process models of agendas with longitudinal data. Neuman's (1990) strategy was to define real-world variation as an important but unmeasured variable and proceed to model the relative response functions of the media and the public. The S-shaped logistic curve, defined as

$$Y = e^x/(1 + e^x)$$

was determined to be "an attractive candidate" for the agenda-setting response function and the analysis specifically used Downs' (1972) notion of the "issue-attention" cycle. Neuman argued that the public perception of most crises does not reflect changes in real conditions as much as the operation of a systematic cycle of heightening public interest followed by a saturation/boredom effect and general public decline of attention.

Downs identified five stages of the issue-attention cycle: (a) *the preproblem stage*—the problem exists but has not captured public attention; (b) *the discovery stage*—here there is a sudden steep ascent of attention and transition from non-problem to problem, which Neuman (1990) termed the *threshold;* (c) *the plateau*—there is a gradual realization that the problem is not easy to solve and that it is quite complex; (d) *the decline*—the public becomes inattentive and possibly frustrated with the problem; and (e) *the postproblem period*—the problem enters a period of inattention, although its objective conditions have not changed significantly as the public awaits a new issue and new hope. In the analysis of the 10 issues, Neuman first "eyeballed" the relationship of the "raw metrics" between the media and public opinion, much like Funkhouser (1973), from which he developed four issue types.

The *crisis category* is exemplified by an issue like Vietnam, which had a clear beginning, middle and end. The drug issue exemplified the *symbolic* crisis as did pollution and poverty, in which a combination of events and the responses of the government, the public, and the media leads to a public definition of the problem of crisis proportions for a limited period of time. The *problem category* is exemplified by an issue like inflation, which is an issue without a story line. Finally, the *nonproblem category* is exemplified by the crime issue, in which there is weak public-opinion effects, moderate media coverage, and a weak relationship between the two (Neuman, 1990). Next, linear regression equations were used to model the slopes of the response functions, with public opinion as the dependent measure and media coverage as the independent measure, although the analysis did not appear to account for stationarity and autocorrelation in the series. There appeared "to be ample evidence indeed that the media and the public have unique dynamics in their response to real-world cues" (p. 172); however, he never examined real-world cues in the model, nor did he account for stationarity and autocorrelation in the models.

Brosius and Kepplinger (1990b) questioned the linearity assumption underlying most of the longitudinal agenda-setting research and derived four alternative nonlinear models of the relationship between media coverage and public opinion. The *threshold* model indicates that a certain threshold of media attention must be met to affect public salience. The *acceleration* model suggests that problem awareness increases or decreases to a larger degree than corresponding media reporting; the same changes in media reporting have different effects on the problem awareness depending on the level of previous reporting and the public reacts more sensitively to issues that are already on the media agenda. The *inertia* model is the reverse of the acceleration model and proposes that problem awareness decreases or increases to a smaller degree than media reporting. Finally, the *echo* model proposes that extraordinary peaks in media reporting have long-term effects on public awareness.

Finally, Brosius and Kepplinger (1990a) investigated static (cross-sectional) and dynamic (longitudinal) approaches to agenda research. In this study, the focus moved from nonlinear modeling to an examination of cause and effect. As in the previous study, regression methods with Granger causality tests were used in which two competing models for the dynamic analysis were tested: media salience leads to public salience versus public salience leads to media salience. The study also attempted to address the issue of nonstationarity. The static analysis revealed nearly no relationship between media coverage and problem awareness, but the dynamic analysis suggested that media coverage caused problem awareness for the issues of energy supply, defense, environmental protection, and European politics. Conversely, problem awareness appeared to cause media coverage for the issues of pensions, public debt, and public security. Significant time lags between 1 and 3 weeks were found for both directions of causality.

ARIMA TIME-SERIES MODELS

In this section, the issues of stationarity and autocorrelation, as well as other components of a time series, are addressed and a method, ARIMA modeling, is presented to model these components in a time-series analysis. Then, several studies that incorporate ARIMA modeling in time-series analyses of agenda setting are examined to develop a methodological foundation for the current analysis of the drug issue.

Autocorrelation and ARIMA Modeling

In ordinary least-squares regression, the following three assumptions are made: (a) the error term has a mean of zero; (b) the error term has a constant variance over all the observations: and (c) the error terms corresponding to different points in time are not correlated. Of the three, the third assumption is often the most important (Ostrom, 1990). When the observations of one variable from different points in time are correlated, the error process is said to be autocorrelated and the third assumption is violated. Autocorrelation in the error term has three primary causes: a misspecified model; omission of important variables, the result of which shows up in the error term; and errors in measurement, which are repeated over time and show up in the error term (McCleary & Hay, 1980). When the third assumption is violated, the estimated regression line fits the data very well, leaving small estimated residuals. Therefore, the estimated variances seriously underestimate the true variances.

The estimated variances are extremely important in the construction of confidence intervals, testing hypotheses, and computing t-ratios. Therefore, when a time series has autocorrelated error terms, the coefficients are unbiased, but the variance and standard deviation are underestimated and tests of significance are inaccurate. In regression analysis, one common method to test for first-order autocorrelation (correlation between successive error terms) is the Durbin–Watson d-statistic (Ostrom, 1990). Some of the agenda-setting studies using time-series regression analysis (e.g., Behr & Iyengar, 1985) use this test for first-order autoregressive processes, and Granger causality tests, in effect, model this first-order autoregressive process into the regression equation. Most time series in the social sciences are first-order autoregressive processes. However, this is a critical assumption because the time series may be a second-order autoregressive process (correlation between the current error term and the two preceding error terms) (McCleary & Hay, 1980; Ostrom, 1990). In addition, a time series contains several other components, such as stationarity, that must be modeled to accurately determine coefficients and test for statistical significance. ARIMA analysis provides a means to model these components.

Although elements of ARIMA modeling can be traced back some 50 years, Box and Jenkins (1976) have been credited with integrating the elements into a comprehensive method, extending it greatly, and popularizing it. ARIMA models posit a random shock, a_t, as the driving force of a time-series process. The most important tenet is that the present input, a_t, will have a greater impact on the present output, Y_t, than any earlier input; that is, the influence of a past event (or input, a_t) diminishes as time passes. ARIMA models, which are based on maximum likelihood estimation, require approximately 40 to 50 time-ordered observations, the interval of which should be constant. Also, the discrete time-series data set should provide an adequate representation of the continuous, underlying process of the variable over time (McCleary & Hay, 1980).

A time series has two basic components: (a) a deterministic component that measures the systematic behavior of a time-series process and is represented by all the parameters of the time series that are not dependent on the error structure; and (b) a stochastic (or "noise") component that describes the underlying process of the unobserved errors, which makes the observed time series somewhat unpredictable. The stochastic component follows certain laws of probability and has two parts: (a) the systematic part—that which is unobserved and is responsible for the autocorrelation in a time series; a major objective of ARIMA analysis is to determine and model the structure of the systematic part of the stochastic component in the corresponding equation so that unbiased estimates of standard deviations can be calculated and correct inferences for the significance tests can be drawn; and (b) the unsystematic part—that which is the unexplained variance left after the systematic part is modeled (McCain & McCleary, 1979).

ARIMA Parameters

ARIMA analysis models three parameters of the systematic part of the stochastic component through the process of identification. These three parameters are the *trend* component (*d*), which addresses the issue of stationarity; the *autoregressive* component (*p*), which addresses the issue of autocorrelation as discussed in the sections on panel studies and correlation and regression in time series; and the *moving average* component (*q*), which is another form of autocorrelation characterized by the persistence of a random shock from one observation to the next. By convention, these parameters are represented as (*p, d, q*) in an ARIMA model.

The first component, trend, is the motion in a specific direction, usually upward or downward, within a series, or, more specifically, any systematic change in the level of a time series (McCleary & Hay, 1980). McCleary and Hay also distinguished between trend and drift:

> The real difference between trend and drift is that trend is deterministic behavior while drift is stochastic behavior.... A time series can drift for extremely long periods of time due only to random forces. Unless there is a strong theoretical basis (or empirical evidence) for assuming that a time series process trends deterministically, there are great advantages to be gained by modeling it stochastically. (pp. 35–36)

Most of the time series used in the social sciences do have systematic trend and are therefore nonstationary in the homogeneous sense. Almost every time series can be made stationary by differencing; that is, by subtracting each observation from the one that follows, for example, the first observation from the second, the second from the third, and the third from the fourth, and so on. Sometimes a second differencing may be required, but this is extremely rare in the social sciences. First-order differencing accounts for the linear trend in the time series; second-order differencing accounts for a quadratic trend. Differencing does not affect the deterministic components of the time series process (McCain & McCleary, 1979). An appropriate differencing procedure always results in a constant series that is represented mathematically as:

$Y_t - Y_{t-1} = \theta_0$ (a constant interpreted as the slope of the series),
or $Y_t = \theta_t$

Finally, although homogenous-sense stationarity is a necessary condition of an ARIMA model, it is not a sufficient condition. An ARIMA model must also have a stationary variance. A process that is stationary in variance will have a single constant variance throughout its course; a series that is not stationary in variance may be made so by transforming the series (e.g., performing a log transformation) after any necessary differencing is implemented (McCleary & Hay, 1980).

The structural parameter p indicates the autoregressive order of an ARIMA (p,d,q) model. Some time series are characterized by a direct relationship between adjacent observations (McCain & McCleary, 1979). The most typical autoregressive process in the social sciences is the first-order autoregressive process, which is represented by an ARIMA (1,0,0) model, or if differenced once by an ARIMA (1,1,0) model,

$$Y_t = \phi y_{t-1} + a_t$$

where f is a correlation coefficient that describes the magnitude of the dependency between adjacent observations and a_t is the error term, or white noise of the process. It is helpful to think of the ARIMA (1,0,0) model as an ordinary least-squares (OLS) regression model in which the current series observation is regressed on the preceding time series observation. Unlike the OLS regression model, the parameter f1 must be constrained to the following interval,

$$-1 < \phi_t < +1,$$

which is termed the bounds of stationarity. The principles of autoregression can also be applied to higher order processes, such as an ARIMA (2,0,0) model, which is a second-order process where the current observation is determined in part by the two preceding observations. Fortunately for previous agenda-setting research that was based on Granger causality which accounted only for first-order autoregression, these second-order processes are not very common in the social sciences, and higher order processes are very rare (McCain & McCleary, 1979).

The white noise, or stochastic component, is the driving force of all ARIMA (p,d,q) models. Integrated (trend) processes are the sum of all the past shocks, or errors, and are well represented by ARIMA (0,d,0) models. Autoregressive processes are an exponentially weighted sum of all past shocks, and are represented by an ARIMA (p,0,0) model. The unifying feature between integrated and autoregressive processes is the persistence of random shock. Each shock persists indefinitely, but for the autoregressive processes the impact of the shock diminishes geometrically.

The final parameter, the moving average process, is characterized by a finite persistence in the random shock. A random shock enters the system and then persists for no more than q observations before it vanishes entirely (McCleary & Hay, 1980). Moving-average processes are represented by ARIMA (0,0,q) models,

$$Y_t = a_t - \theta_1 a_{t-1}$$

where θ is a correlation coefficient and a_t is an error term. The general principle of the moving average process is that a random shock persists for exactly θ observations and then is gone. In moving average process, θ must be constrained as follows:

$$-1 < \theta < +1$$

which is called the bounds of invertability. As with autoregressive processes, higher order processes are possible (0,0,2), but they are very rare in the social sciences (McCleary & Hay, 1980).

In theory, a time series can have both an autoregressive and a moving average term (McCain & McCleary, 1979). For example, an ARIMA (1,1,1) describes a differenced model where the current observation, Y_t, is predicted from both the preceding past observation, Y_{t-1}, and the preceding random shock, a_{t-1}. (Mixed processes are rarely found in the social sciences, but in theory they exist).

In addition, a series can have seasonal components in the ARIMA model, or seasonal cycles that must be incorporated into the stochastic component. As an example, there are two types of autocorrelation: regular autocorrelation, described earlier as the structural dependency among adjacent observations; and seasonal autocorrelation, described as the structural dependency among observations separated by one period or cycle, such as an annual cycle or 6 month cycle (McCain & McCleary, 1979). The seasonal structural parameters are denoted by upper-case letters: P specifies the number of seasonal autoregressive terms; D specifies the number of times a series must be seasonally differenced; Q specifies the number of seasonal moving-average terms; and S denotes the length or order of the period or cycle. The conventional means for specifying a seasonal model is ARIMA (p,d,q) (P,D,Q)$_s$ (McCleary & Hay, 1980; see Appendix B for additional information on ARIMA modeling).

ARIMA Modeling and Agenda-Setting Research

ARIMA modeling is a relatively new methodological approach in agenda-setting research. Currently, only a few studies have employed this method, such as Rogers et al.'s (1991) examination of the AIDS issue (also see Dearing, 1989; and Gonzenbach, 1992). This study provides the methodological heart of this book's analysis of the relationships among the drug-issue agendas.

The study by Rogers et al. (1991) examined the relationships among five agendas over 91 consecutive monthly time intervals: the polling agenda, as represented by the number of polls about the issue; the science agenda, as represented by the frequency of monthly articles in four leading medical journals; the real-world cue measure, which has the number of monthly AIDS cases; the media's agenda, comprising the monthly frequency of stories from *The New York Times*, the *Washington Post*, the *Los Angeles Times*, and the three networks' evening news broadcasts; and the policy agenda, which was the average monthly federal expenditures for AIDS research, education, and testing created from the annual expenditures for the years of the study.

Each of the univariate series was modeled with ARIMA modeling, and then the modeled series were used in a Granger causality test to determine whether causal relationships existed between each of the 10 possible pairs of relationships (Rogers et al., 1991). Granger causality is frequently used to determine over-time causality in longitudinal data. As K. A. Smith (1987) noted, X is a Granger cause of Y when Y is better predicted by incorporating X's past history over and above the influence of Y's past history on itself.

Rogers et al. (1991) specified the following possible conclusions for the Granger causality test:

1. A one-way causal relationship is determined when one time series explains the other, but the reverse does not occur.
2. A feedback, or reciprocal causal relationship, occurs when two time series contribute equally to explain each other's variance when they are included in the regression equation of the other.
3. An instantaneous causal link occurs when the present and the past history of one time series contributes to increase the other variable's total variance explained.
4. The absence of Granger causality is assessed when neither of two series increase the other's variance by including their past histories for the other. (pp. 26–27)

Four of the possible 10 pairs showed one-way causality over the 91-month time series: The science agenda predicted the media agenda; the number of AIDS cases predicted the media agenda; the science agenda predicted the polling agenda; and the policy agenda predicted the polling agenda. One pair, the media and polling relationship, showed a reciprocal, two-way relationship. The five significant bivariate relationships had two common dependent series, the media agenda and the polling agenda. The significant predictors from the bivariate analyses were then used to test two multivariate models, one with the media agenda as the dependent series and the other with the polling agenda as the dependent series. This analysis utilized multivariate transfer function analysis (Cuddington, 1980).

The first model indicated that the media agenda was predicted by itself, the science agenda, the polling agenda, and the number of AIDS cases. The second model indicated the polling agenda was predicted by itself, the media agenda, and the policy agenda. Finally, they repeated the steps of the aforementioned analysis for each of the four eras of the AIDS issue, which they had determined from a content analysis of the issue: the initial era (23 months), the science era (26 months), the human era (19 months), and the political era (23 months). As noted previously, this analysis may be suspect given the very low number of time intervals used in these four separate analyses (see McCleary & Hay, 1980).

CONCLUSION

This chapter specifically examines the major methodological approaches used to examine agendas and agenda-setting relationships over time. Agenda-setting process research presents many methodological problems concerning the measurement of agendas and agenda relationships over time, and the methodological approaches have grown with the emerging time-series databases and methodological techniques. The methodological progression in agenda-setting research has moved from cross-sectional studies to more sophisticated research designs that allow more precise exploration of agenda setting as a process. This methodological progression can be categorized into cross-sectional studies, trend studies, panel designs, and time-series designs.

Although agenda setting is, by definition, a time-related process, many of the early agenda-setting studies relied on cross-sectional data, which, by definition, cannot directly capture the relationships of the agendas over time. A cross-sectional study's static design cannot account fully for the dynamic nature of the agenda-setting process, nor can it account at all for time lags of possible effects. The early agenda-setting research focused too narrowly on short time frames because the researchers came from an effects tradition,

A trend study is based on measures from successive samples from the same population at different points in time in which the researcher examines the change in the variable over time. In agenda-setting research, the trend analysis' key weakness is that researchers have generally "eyeballed" the trend over time with rather simple graphic representations or applied analytic methods that do not adequately address the often complex mathematical nature of the time-series processes. However, these early studies make an important contribution to agenda-setting research in that they seek to examine the agenda-setting process over long periods of time and to disentangle the complexities of relationships of issue agendas over time.

Panel and time-series designs examine the differences between units in patterns of change, or determine the effects of a change in one variable on another variable. The investigation of such questions is aided by the collection of data at more than one point in time on the same units of analysis. The most commonly used design is the time series, for which observations are collected on a single individual or other unit of analysis for a large number of time intervals; a second common method is the panel study, in which observations are collected for a number of individuals (or other units of analysis) instead of only one, at two or more points in time. In agenda-setting research, the major difference between the two is that in a panel study the unit of analysis is the individual, who is typically surveyed at only a few points in time; in a time-series analysis, the unit of analysis is typically an aggregate measure. The typical time-series study usually includes numerous time points. Time-series studies use two methods: The first type uses correlation and regression methods to examine the time-series process; the second type uses ARIMA models to mathematically model the various time-series components.

It is best to think of a time series as a mathematically alive entity. It has two primary "alive" components that must be mathematically modeled. The first, *stationarity,* means that time series has no secular trend, or that there is no systematic increase or decrease in the level of the series as it drifts upwards or downwards over time. The second, *autocorrelation* means that observations of one variable from different points in time are correlated, or some observation Y_t (an observation in a series at some point in time) is predicted by a previous observation in the series Y_{t-1}. Many of the early agenda-setting, time-series studies did not adequately model these components; however, recent ARIMA-based studies have addressed these issues and have provided a foundation to adequately examine the relationships of agendas over time.

Conceptual Considerations and Measures

The objective of this study is to examine the drug issue from mid-1984 to mid-1991 to determine how drug-related issues and events, both real and fabricated, and the primary agendas drove the issue over time. Agenda setting provides an important theoretical foundation to examine how the media and president interpret and restructure issue and event information over time and to determine how the various agendas interact over time to drive an issue through time.

This chapter first specifies the study's four research questions and the specific hypotheses to be tested. Second, it describes the specific methodologies that will be used to address the research questions and hypotheses. Third, a detailed description is offered about how the various drug-issue agendas are operationalized for the time-series analysis.

RESEARCH QUESTIONS

The study proposes four research questions concerning the drug issue:

1. *The media's structuring of issues and events.* How did the media structure interpretations and presentations of issue and event information over time?

2. *The President's structuring of issues and events.* How did the president structure public relations interpretations and presentations of issue and event information over time?

3. *The relationships of the agendas over time.* What were the interactions of the drug-issue agendas of the president, the media, and the public, while controlling for the policy agenda and a real-world measure of the severity of the drug problem? Based on previous research, most specifically Gonzenbach's 1992 study, we propose the following hypotheses (see Fig. 3.1). First, a two-way effect will occur

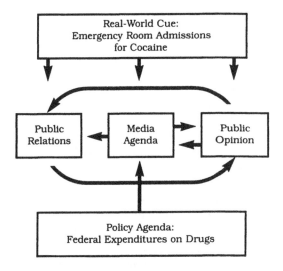

FIG. 3.1. Agenda-setting model for drug issue analysis.

between the media agenda and public opinion, but the media-to-opinion effect will occur more quickly (with a shorter lag) than the opinion-to-media effect. Second, a two-way effect will occur between the public-relations agenda and public opinion, but the public-relations-to-opinion effect will occur more quickly (with a shorter lag) than the opinion-to-public-relations effect. Third, the media agenda will have a one-way effect on the public relations agenda. Fourth, the policy agenda will have a one-way effect on the media agenda. The real-world cue will have a one-way effect on the public relations agenda, the media agenda, and public opinion.

The theoretical findings also suggest the following hypotheses: (a) the real-world cue will have a one-way effect on the policy agenda; (b) the public relations agenda and public opinion will have a one-way effect on the policy agenda; and (c) a two-way effect will occur between the media agenda and the policy agenda, but the policy-to-media effect will occur more quickly than the media-to-policy effect. However, due to limitations in the data, as noted later, it was not possible to treat the real-world cue measure and the policy agenda as dependent series in this analysis. Therefore, these hypotheses were not tested in this study.

4. *Relationships of agendas in the two administrations.* How did the relationships of these agendas differ during the Reagan and Bush presidencies? Based on the analysis of the two presidents' public-relations agendas, President Bush appeared to be a much more active president concerning the drug issue, and therefore it is tentatively predicted that there will be a greater difference in the agenda-setting process between the two administrations. It is also predicted that President Bush was more influenced by the public, the media, and real-world cues than was President Reagan.

METHOD

The first research question concerning the media's structuring of issues and events is examined by a content analysis of the issues and events of the drug issue (Lichter & Lichter, 1990; Rogers & Dearing, 1988; Shaw, 1977). The content analysis is used to descriptively determine various stages of media coverage according to Downs' (1972) issue-attention cycle model (also see Neuman, 1990). Next, the issue and event coverage for each stage is descriptively compared to the total media coverage of each stage to gauge what issues and events were structuring the media's coverage for each stage. The content analysis was conducted solely by the author of the study.

Two measures of intercoder reliability were used to determine the reliability of the coding: Scott's (1955) pi and Holsti's (1969) reliability test. Eight randomly selected months, one from each of the years of the study, were coded twice at different time intervals by the author. The reliability tests were limited to the issue and event variables in that variables such as month and medium (network television vs. *The Times*) presented no coding problems. A total of 923 stories, or 9% of all stories, were used in the reliability tests. The Scott's pi was .942 (a standard acceptable level is .75) and the Holsti reliability measure was .953 (an acceptable level is .90).

The second research question concerning the president's structuring of issues and events is the same as the media content analysis; however, the content analysis was based on the Public Papers of the Presidents (see description later) and the reliability tests are based on all coded materials. The Scott's pi was .874 and the Holsti reliability measure was .913.

The third research question, the relationships of the agendas over time, and its specific hypotheses, are examined with ARIMA modeling, bivariate Granger causality tests, and a multivariate analysis utilizing Yule-Walker estimation. Each of the five time series (media agenda, presidential public-relations agenda, public agenda, the policy agenda, and a real-world cue measure) are identified, estimated, and diagnosed with ARIMA modeling. The bivariate relationships between the series, each of which is prewhitened with the Haugh-Box (1977) method, are then tested for Granger causality with a regression procedure using Yule–Walker estimation (SAS Institute, 1988). Finally, based on Granger causality, the significant series are then tested in several multivariate models, again using Haugh-Box prewhitening and Yule-Walker estimation.

The fourth research question, the relationships of agendas in the Reagan and Bush administrations, is examined with the same procedure as the second; however, the models are examined controlling for the time frames of the respective administrations: Reagan, July 1984–December 1988; Bush, January 1988–June 1991.

DATA

The study comprises five agenda measures for each of the months of the study, July 1984 to June 1991, or a total of 84 monthly time points. The *public-opinion* measure comprises the American public's monthly opinion of drugs as the country's most important problem. The *media agenda* comprises the monthly frequency of drug stories in *The New York Times* and the three nightly network news broadcasts. The *presidential public-relations agenda* comprises the monthly frequency of public statements about the drug issue by Presidents Reagan and Bush in the Public Papers of the Presidents. The *real-world cue* measures the real-world severity of the drug problem with monthly measures of the number of cocaine-related emergency-room admissions. Finally, the *policy agenda* comprises monthly estimates of the federal government's expenditures for the drug problem.

Public Opinion

The public-opinion measure was created by compiling monthly national polls in which similar versions of the question "What do you think is the most important problem facing the country today?" were asked. Ninety-three monthly polls from 13 different survey organizations are used to determine public opinion for 60 of the 84 months of the study, and 24 months are estimated by interpolation (see Appendix A). The 93 polls represent the 13 different survey organizations with the following frequencies: Gallup, 24; Cambridge Reports, 23; CBS/*New York Times,* 19; ABC/Washington *Post,* 8; NBC/*Wall Street Journal,* 4; Los Angeles *Times,* 3; Yankelovich, Clancy, and Schulman, 3; ABC, 2; Associate Press/Media General, 2; Washington *Post,* 2; CBS, 1; *New York Times,* 1; Princeton Survey Research Associates, 1.

All of the surveys were based on national samples of adults; 67 were conducted by phone, and 26 were based on personal interviews. A comparison of the two methods for months with both methods included indicated no significant differences in the responses for the two methods. All of the surveys used very similar versions of the aforementioned question; however, five of the surveys used a closed-question format.

According to Schuman and Scott (1987), closed questions can "sharply restrict frames of reference by focusing attention on the alternatives offered, no matter how impoverished those alternatives may be and no matter how much effort is made to offer respondents freedom to depart from them" (p. 957). Thus, we adjusted these "closed" surveys. Four of these were NBC/*Wall Street Journal* surveys and one was a Yankelovich survey. Four of the five closed-end surveys were given in months that also included surveys with open-ended, single-response surveys. An adjustment factor (.43) was derived from these 4 months by dividing the "open" percentage by the "closed" percentage. This factor was then applied to all five of the "closed" surveys. In addition, all of the Cambridge Report surveys specifically asked for "first" and "second" choices. Of the 23 Cambridge Report surveys we used, 11 had the responses separated into "first" and "second" responses, whereas 12 had them grouped together. An adjustment factor (.524) was created to adjust the 12 unseparated Cambridge Report polls by dividing the "first" choices percentages by the "total" percentages (first and second choices) from the 11 separated surveys and then using this adjustment factor to estimate the "first" response for the 12 unseparated surveys.

Of the 93 surveys, 64 did not accept multiple responses, whereas 29 did. These 29 multiple-response surveys were adjusted by dividing the percentage response by the total percentage of the survey. For example, if 20% said drugs were the most important problem, and the total survey responses were 120%, the 20 was divided by 120, thus giving 16.6% who considered drugs to be the most important problem. (For a discussion of this method, see Behr & Iyengar, 1985.)

The range of the sample sizes for the 93 surveys is 500 to 4,244, with a mean of 1,380 and a standard deviation of 469. The mean for the midpoint of when the polls were conducted during the month was 14.76 with a standard deviation of 7.3 days. The Cambridge Report surveys used a sample size of between 1,405 and 1,550 respondents; the exact sample sizes were not available from the surveys nor from the organization's data librarian. Thus we used the minimum in our calculations. The exact dates of the Cambridge Reports were also not available from the surveys. The data librarian indicated that day 15 of the month of the polls was a very good estimate based on his experiences with the scheduling of these surveys. Therefore, our midpoint estimates use this day for our midpoint calculations.

The public-opinion measure for May 1988 is based on the mean of two polls: ABC/Washington *Post* (26%) and CBS/*New York Times* (16%). This was the only month in which we found two open-ended questions with significantly different responses, so we created a mean response of 21% from the two polls.

This study is an exploratory investigation that uses a rather novel, quilted picture of public opinion over time, comprising various sources of public opinion measurement. The hope is to paint a rather large picture of the shadows of the reality of public opinion about the drug issue during this time to guide future research, and the various sources of errors, such as "house" effects, midpoint variance, and estimation error, are fully acknowledged in these quilted measures. The methodology offers promise for other research and provides an important contribution relative to the alternative of avoiding time-series analysis because of insufficient measures.

Media Agenda

The media-agenda measure comprises the monthly frequency of articles about the drug issue in *The New York Times* and the three networks' nightly news broadcasts from July 1984 to June 1991. The measure is a census of all stories from these sources and was created by a content analysis of *The New York Times Index* and the *Vanderbilt Archives News Abstracts*. *The New York Times* was chosen to represent the newspaper agenda for several reasons. It is the elite U.S. newspaper (Winter & Eyal, 1981) and is a model from which the television networks derive their news judgments. In addition, *The New York Times'* coverage was more strongly related to measures of public concern about the drug issue than was that of any other medium (Shoemaker et al., 1989). However, as noted by Rogers et al. (1991), we also believed it was important to represent the "national" picture of the drug issue offered by the networks, and therefore, like Rogers et al., we created a cumulative media measure comprising the frequency of stories from both *The New York Times* and the television networks.

The frequency of stories about illegal drugs was used for pragmatic reasons: The time and costs of estimating column inches or measuring the number of words per story would have been prohibitive. In addition, research indicates that frequency may be as strong a measure as column inches. Stone and McCombs (1981) found a Pearson correlation coefficient of +.90 between the number of stories and the number of column inches devoted to a variety of topics. A census of stories was used instead of a sample of stories to insure adequate monthly figures for the analysis.

Presidential Public-Relations Agenda

The presidential-agenda measure was created by a content analysis of the monthly frequency of public releases made by the presidents about the drug issue from July 1984 to June 1991. A computer-based analysis was conducted of the Public Papers of the Presidents, which provides the text of the president's public remarks, proclamations, statements, and releases. This measure provides a good indicator of the president's drug agenda in that it measures the relative emphasis of the president's public relations efforts to communicate messages to the public about the issue. The frequency measure was used for the same reasons as that of media agenda. The computer search of the presidential papers used the following search strategy to avoid picking up any possible stories about legal drugs: drug abuse, drug traffic, drug smuggling, illegal drugs, drug policy, drug czar, cocaine, heroin, marijuana.

Real-World Cue Measure

The real-world cue measure comprises the frequency of hospital emergency-room episodes involving cocaine for each annual quarter from the third quarter of 1984 through the second quarter of 1991. The data are from the National Institute of Drug

Abuse's (NIDA) Drug Abuse Warning Network and are limited to the hospitals that consistently report quarterly reports to avoid inconsistency in the results from irregularly reporting hospitals. The hospital emergency-room episodes were used instead of some other alternatives because they tend to avoid variations due to policy. As an example, arrest rates are innately biased toward the lower economic groups, and the quantity of drugs being imported sometimes reflects political interests, depending on the agency reporting the results. The emergency-room measure seems to avoid some of those problems, at least according to sources from NIDA. In addition, the episodes regarding cocaine were used because, unlike heroin/morphine and marijuana, the data included variance over time and represented, in our opinion, a better picture of the driving source of the drug problem—cocaine and crack cocaine (Johnston, 1989).

Several adjustments had to be made to the data. The original quarterly data were obtained from NIDA's September 1990 file of the Drug Abuse Warning Network as presented in remarks made by Louis W. Sullivan, MD, secretary of Health and Human Services, at a press conference held at the White House on December 19, 1990 (see Sullivan, 1990). This report included quarterly data from the third quarter of 1985 through the second quarter of 1990. We obtained data directly from NIDA for the last two quarters of 1984 and the first two quarters of 1985; however, complications arose regarding the data from the third quarter of 1990 through the second quarter of 1991.

In a conversation with the head of NIDA's Statistical Analysis and Population Survey Section, Division of Epidemiology and Prevention Research (Gfroerer, personal communication, 1992), we were told that a new weighting procedure had been developed and had been applied to the data from the beginning of 1988 to the present that we were given. However, NIDA was not able to release the weighting procedure due to technical reasons. Therefore, we had unweighted data only from the third quarter of 1984 through the second quarter of 1990, both unweighted and weighted data from the first quarter of 1988 through the second quarter of 1990, and weighted data only from the third quarter of 1990 through the second quarter of 1991. A regression model using the data from the periods in which both unweighted and weighted data was available was thus used to predict the unweighted from the weighted data.

The equation for the model, with an explained variance of .91 was:

Unweighted = 369 + .374 x Weighted

This model was then used to estimate the unweighted figures for the third quarter of 1990 through the second quarter of 1991, in that most of the data was unweighted. The quarterly data derived from this method was then divided by 3 to estimate the monthly figures for this measure. Given the estimation procedure for the monthly data, it was judged imprudent to use the measure as a dependent series. Therefore, the variable is used only as an independent series in the analysis.

Policy Agenda

The policy agenda measures the annual federal expenditures on the drug issue from 1984 to 1990. The Office of National Drug Control Policy (1991) provided a breakdown of expenditures in the following categories: interdiction, investigation, international, prosecution, corrections, intelligence, state and local assistance, research and development, regulatory and compliance, other law enforcement, drug abuse prevention, and drug abuse treatment. This study uses the aggregate annual figures for all of these categories; that is, all federal expenditure on illegal drugs. Given the time frame of the study, the annual expenditures were converted to constant dollars. Munn, Garcia, and Woelfel (1991) suggested five alternative methods for constant dollar conversion: the gross national product deflator, the consumer price index for urban dwellers, the wholesale price index, the composite construction index, and the commodity price index. The consumer price index for urban dwellers was used for this analysis, and converts the expenditures into 1967 dollars. Like Rogers et al. (1991), the assumption is made that the annual expenditures are allotted equally across the months of each fiscal year, and thus use a monthly average for the months of each respective year for July 1984 through June 1991. As with the real-world cue measure, it was judged imprudent to use the measure as a dependent series because of the monthly estimation procedure. Therefore, the variable is used only as an independent series in the analysis.

Chapter **4**

The Media's Structuring of the Drug Issue

This chapter examines the first research question; namely, how did the media structure interpretations and presentations of issue and event information over time? If journalists do not have new information about an issue, news coverage will stop. This new information is necessary for news gatekeepers to consider an "old" issue newsworthy, and the new information must allow journalists to restructure the issue in a new light (Rogers et al., 1991). The analysis examines and integrates three aspects of the media's coverage of the drug issue from 1984 to 1991 to determine how new information and the changing media interpretations of the information about the issue of illegal drugs defined and drove the issue through time.

First, the news reports are classified into issue and event categories based respectively on the conceptualizations of Lichter and Lichter (1990) and Shaw (1977). Second, the cycle of media coverage, based on the monthly frequency of news reports, is plotted and examined in relation to Downs' (1972) issue–attention cycle to determine if the media's coverage is represented by Downs' model. Third, the frequency structure of key issues and events is contrasted against the frequency structure of total media coverage for the respective stages of Downs' issue–attention cycle to determine if and when these key issues and events "drive" the structure of coverage for the respective stages.

MEDIA CONTENT

From July 1984 to June 1991, *The New York Times* presented 7,462 articles about the drug issue, and the three networks aired 2,600 stories on the evening news, for a total of 10,062 stories. *The New York Times* and the network news appeared to give the same relative emphasis to coverage of the issue over time in terms of the frequency of coverage.

The important issue for this analysis is the nature of the coverage. An important way to conceptualize an issue is to distinguish issues from events (Shaw, 1977). An event is a discrete happening that is limited by space and time, and an issue is cumulative news coverage of a series of related events that fit together in a broad category or "specific components of issues" (Rogers & Dearing, 1987, p. 566). Using these definitions, the drug problem in the United States is by itself the large issue of coverage; within this broad issue, however, the media are shining their spotlight on specific events that loosely combine into broader subissues, or issues of the drug issue. The combination of these events and subissues therefore defines the content of the drug issue or problem. To determine these drug events and drug subissues, henceforth referred to as drug issues, a content analysis was conducted of the 10,062 news reports in *The New York Times* and the early evening news broadcasts of ABC, NBC, and CBS for the period of the study (see Fig. 4.1).

The content analysis categorized the stories both in terms of their issue and event content. The issue categorization was based generally on a categorization of drug issues presented by Lichter and Lichter (1990). The event categorization comprised a categorization of 98 unique events concerning the drug problem.

ISSUES OF THE DRUG ISSUE

The content analysis of the issues of the drug problem is comprised of 10 general issue categories, which subsume 28 specific issue categories. The 10 general issue categories are: use and demand (19%), supply (3%), enforcement/interest group activities (22%), judicial (16%), administrative activity (17%), policy options (10%), helping victims (9%); public opinion and concern (1%), political use of the drug issue (1%), and miscellaneous (1%). The analysis in this chapter uses 28 specific issue categories, which are defined in Table 4.1.

The major issues (see Fig. 4.2) are coverage of those court cases that are drug-related, which accounts for 16% of all coverage, followed by stories about the violence and crime related to drugs, which account for 10% of all coverage. These issues, combined with U. S. administrative activities (8%), testing (7%), and drug busts (7%), account for almost 50% of the coverage. Over the period of the study the media gave a heavy focus to the government's control of the users and dealers of drugs.

Generally, the media covered the 28 issues in a very similar manner with the exception of international administration, business enforcement, treatment, and AIDS (see Fig. 4.3). Television used 10% of its coverage for international administration coverage, and print used only 5%. In addition, television gave 5% of its coverage to military use, whereas print gave 2%. Conversely, print focused slightly more on business enforcement (4% vs. 1%), treatment (3% vs. 1%), and AIDS (3% vs. 1%). These minor differences suggest that television may focus more on the international angle of the issue, whereas print may focus a little more on the domestic concerns. However, the two media generally covered the issue in a very similar fashion.

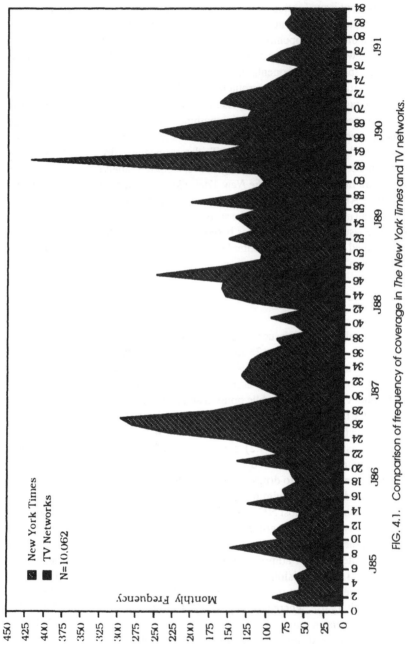

FIG. 4.1. Comparison of frequency of coverage in *The New York Times* and TV networks.

TABLE 4.1
Media Content Analysis Categories

Use and Demand

Profiles of users/dealers: articles examining individual users and purveyors of illegal drugs.
Demand for drugs: articles about the demand for drugs.
Violence/crime: articles about violence and criminal activities related to drug use and sales.
Children as victims: articles about the effect of drugs on children, including drug use and pregnancy issues.

Supply

Foreign sources of drugs: articles about the importation of drugs into the United States from foreign countries.
Domestic sources of drugs: articles about the domestic sources of drugs.
New drugs: articles about new drugs and strains of drugs that increase demand options.

Enforcement/Interest Group Activities

U.S. enforcement activity: articles about activities by U.S. enforcement agencies (federal, state, and local: not including the military) to stop the influx and use of domestic and foreign drugs, not including articles about specific drug busts.
Military enforcement operations: activities by the U.S. military, including the Coast Guard, to stop the importation of drugs.
Foreign enforcement activity: articles about activities of foreign enforcement agencies to stop use, supply, and exportation of drugs.
Unofficial groups: articles about unofficial public interest groups to stop the use and supply of drugs.
Business and education: articles about the activities of businesses, industries, and educational institutions to stop the use and supply of drugs.

Judicial Activities

Court cases: articles about specific court cases concerning drug arrests and issues.
Drug busts: articles about specific arrests of drug dealers and users.

Administrative Activities

U.S. administrative: articles about activities of U.S. administrative and legislative agencies (nonenforcement) concerning the drug issue, not related to specific court cases or arrests.
International administrative: articles about the administrative relationship between the U.S. and foreign government(s) concerning the supply and demand of drugs.
Foreign administrative: articles about the administrative activities of foreign governments concerning the supply and demand of drugs.

Policy Options

Sentencing and penalties: articles about specific options for sentencing and drug-related penalties not concerning specific court cases.
Funding: articles examining specific federal, state, and local funding issues concerning drugs.
Testing: articles specifically examining drug-testing options, implementation, and issues.
Legalization: articles about the legalization of drugs as a policy option.

Helping Victims

Treatment and rehabilitation: articles about treatment/rehabilitation initiatives, programs and actions.
Education and prevention: articles about initiatives, programs, and efforts to educate people about the negative effects of drugs.
Scientific research: articles about research concerning drugs, not including research concerning demand issues.
Drugs and AIDS: articles about the relationship drug use and AIDS.

Public Opinion and Concern

Public opinion and concern: articles about the public's reaction to the drug issue, including articles about public-opinion polls.

Political Use of the Drug Issue

Political use of the drug issue: articles about political candidates' use of the drug issue in elections and political conflicts.

Miscellaneous

Other: articles that do not fit into any of the aforementioned categories concerning the drug issue.

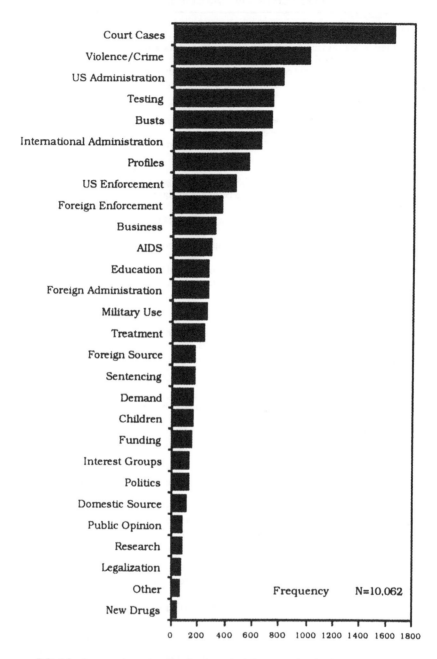

FIG. 4.2. Issue categories: Content analysis frequencies for *The New York Times* and TV networks.

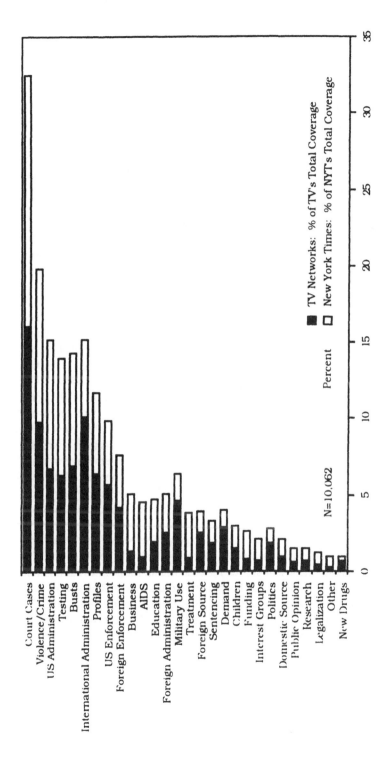

FIG. 4.3. Issue categories: Percentage of total coverage for *The New York Times* and TV networks.

EVENTS OF THE DRUG ISSUE

In the content analysis, 3,831 of the 10,062 stories were coded into specific event categories concerning discrete happenings related to drugs. These event categories generally cross over into several issue categories; for example, the events surrounding the kidnapping and death of Enrique Camarena Salazar fell into several issue categories, including violence and crime, international administration, and foreign enforcement. The events, in some cases, may have a slightly broad focus. The sports event category, for example, actually comprises numerous subevents. However, these event categories often have a significant impact on the public, as exemplified by recent docudramas about Salazar and the United States involvement with Colombia and the significant impact of the death of Len Bias (Merriam, 1989).

In the content analysis, 98 event categories were coded and the 15 most frequently covered events examined (see Fig. 4.4). Sports events comprised 9% of all coverage. Although the death of Len Bias can be considered a sports-related event, it is treated as a separate event given the significance of this death (Merriam, 1989). Articles about the Colombian drug connection accounted for 5% of all media coverage, followed closely by the arrest and trial of Manuel Noriega (3%) and Mayor Marion Barry of Washington, DC (2%). The death of Salazar and coverage of Mexican-related drug problems accounted for about 1% each of the total coverage, as did U.S. government concerns about transportation workers using drugs and the death of Len Bias. The "pizza connection" drug trial in New York and John deLorean's drug-related adventures captured slightly less than 1% of the coverage of each. U.S. government concern about government employees' drug use and coverage of efforts by schools to control drugs each comprised a little less than 1% of the coverage, and finally, Bush's drug plan, coverage of the drug czar, and discussion of a war against drugs all accounted for slightly less than 1% of the coverage each.

Figure 4.5 examines the differences in coverage of The New York Times and the broadcast media concerning the event categories. It should be noted that the figure comprises the frequency of stories for each media for each event and not the column percentage. This was done because the column percentages were very small in many of the categories. In that television coverage comprises 26% of the total coverage, and print comprises 74%, the ratio should be approximately 1:3 when contrasting television with print if there is no difference in the amount of coverage. In general, television focused heavily on the events of the drug problem. Television coverage is disproportionately heavy in its coverage of the event categories of Colombia, Salazar, Mexico, deLorean, and President Bush's drug plan, whereas print is disproportionately heavy in its coverage of sports and the

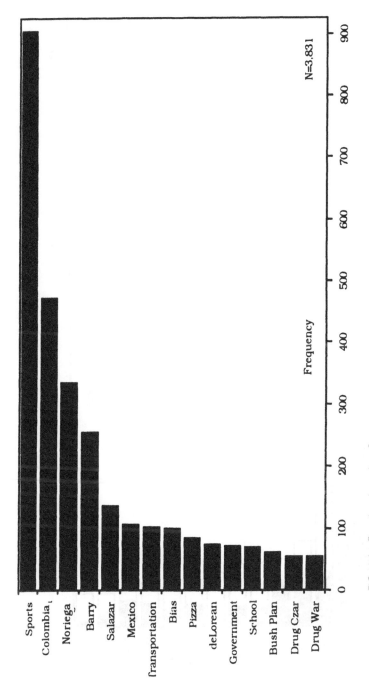

FIG. 4.4. Event categories: Content analysis frequencies for *The New York Times* and TV networks.

42

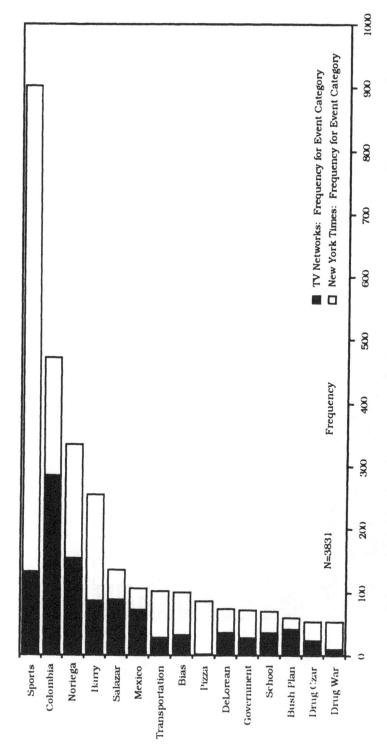

FIG. 4.5.   Event categories: Frequency of coverage for *The New York Times* and TV networks.

"pizza connection" drug ring. Given the space allotted to sports in *The New York Times* and the local nature of the "pizza" event, the figures seem logical.

THE CYCLE OF COVERAGE

When media coverage is plotted over time, the plot is usually a recurring (and sometimes exponential in growth) cycle, with each cycle, or portion of the cycle, representing a restructuring of the issue via event information. "The over-time content of the media coverage of an issue represents not only new information, but also periodic changes in how journalists, editors, and hence viewers and readers interpret the old issue in light of new information" (Rogers et al., 1991, pp. 3–4). In a similar light, Downs' (1972) issue-attention cycle, although directed at the effects of information on the public, can also be applied to the media's perception of a problem in that the personnel of the media are a public with a highly focused sense of attention to problems.

Downs identified five stages of the issue-attention cycle: (a) *the preproblem stage*—the problem exists but has not captured public attention; (b) *the discovery stage*—there is a sudden steep ascent of attention and transition from nonproblem to problem; (c) *the plateau*—there is a gradual realization that the problem is not easy to solve and that it is quite complex; (d) *the decline*—the public becomes inattentive and possibly frustrated with the problem; and (e) *the postproblem period*—the problem enters a period of inattention, although its objective conditions have not changed significantly as the public awaits a new issue and new hope (Neuman, 1990). In this section, the media's coverage is examined to determine the cyclical pattern of the media's restructuring of the drug issue and the possible categorization of these cycles in relation to Down's (1972) conceptualization of the issue–attention cycle.

A content analysis of national media coverage of the drug issue between 1983 and 1987 indicated "a classic pattern: there was a slow initial increase in overall media attention, followed by a shift in emphasis to subject matters of broader interest. Then interest in drugs increased sharply, peaked and declined" (Merriam, 1989, p. 21). Media coverage from mid-1984 to mid-1991 appears to follow a similar pattern (see Fig. 4.6).

Preproblem Stage: July 1984–May 1986

In the period from July 1984 to May 1986, the coverage of the drug issue by *The New York Times* and the networks fluctuated mildly around an average number of stories of 79 per month. This appears to equate with Downs' categorization of the preproblem stage of an issue, in which a problem exists, as indicated by the

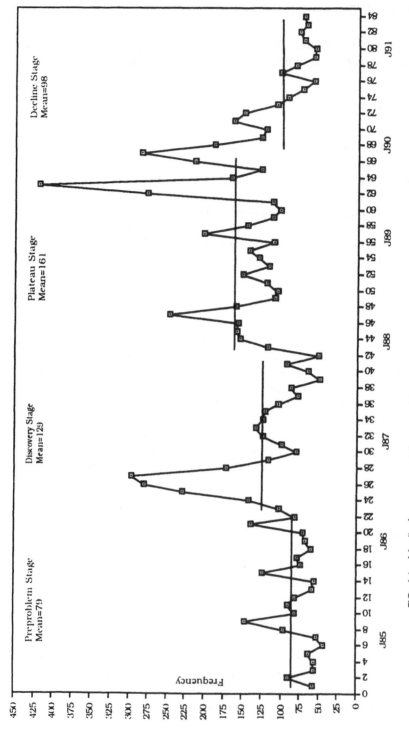

FIG. 4.6. Media frequency and means of four stages of the media content cycle: July 1984–June 1991.

44

introduction of crack cocaine (Johnston, 1989) but has not captured the public's (in this case the media's) attention.[1]

In the period from June to October of 1986, the media's coverage of the issue peaked, with 280 stories in August and 297 stories in September. After this September peak, the frequency of coverage declined to preproblem-stage levels until January 1988, when coverage began a second surge. The June-to-October increase in coverage was driven by strong public information campaigns by NIDA ("Cocaine, The Big Lie") that began in April, political interests in the 1986 election, Len Bias' death in June, and President Reagan's war on drugs, which he emphasized between August and October of 1986 (Merriam, 1989). *The New York Times* suggested that Reagan's short-lived war had died down rapidly after the great deal of activity in the second half of 1986.

Discovery Stage: June 1986–December 1987

The period from June 1986 to December 1987 averaged 129 stories per month, a marked increase compared to the preproblem period. The second phase of coverage in the media cycle indicated a *discovery* stage in media coverage—there is a sudden steep ascent of attention and transition from nonproblem to problem. (See comments by Merriam, chapter 1, this volume.) (1989), "Bias' death posed an almost media-perfect example of the dangers of drug overdose…concern for his death matched closely with the concerns national media and government leaders were seeking to present" (p. 21).

Plateau Stage: January 1988–January 1990

The period from January 1988 to January 1990 is marked by four sharp peaks in coverage. The first, in May 1988, is comprised of 247 stories. The second, March 1989, is not quite as sharp, but still includes 201 stories. The third, September 1989,

---

[1]In the analysis of the four stages, several methods were used in an attempt to quantitatively separate the stages. First, the Chow test (Rogers et al., 1991) was used to examine differences between the respective stages and numerous other possibilities. Following is a summary of the F-Tests contrasting the stages: Stages 1 and 2: $F = 24.67$ $df = 2,38$ (significant); Stages 2 and 3: $F = 7.67$ $df = 2,39$ (n.s.); Stages 3–4: $F = 6.12$ $df = 2,37$ (n.s.). We also attempted to use ARIMA transfer function models, again to no avail. Finally, we plotted the regression slope for each stage to contrast the movement of the respective series. Following is a summary that indicates fairly strong differences in the tendencies of the slopes, which we consider adequate evidence, in conjunction with the shifts in content and frequency, to categorize the four stages:

Stage 1 (Months 1–23): $y = 63.9 + 1.3x$
Stage 2 (Months 24–42): $y = 438.7 - 9.4x$
Stage 3 (Months 42–67): $y = -34.9 + 3.6x$
Stage 4 (Months 68–84): $y = 571.2 - 6.2x$

represents the pinnacle of media attention in the cycle with 419 stories. The fourth, January 1990, comprises 285 stories. The entire stage has a mean frequency of stories of 161.

According to Downs (1972), this phase of the issue–attention cycle should be marked by a gradual realization that the problem is not easy to solve and that it is quite complex. In many ways this appears to be true for the media's attempt to focus on the many problems and approaches to solving the drug problem represented in this phase. The media appeared to be in a cyclic "feeding frenzy" of coverage during this period; however, unlike Downs' conceptualization of issue complexity, the sources of many of the stories in this stage—the president and the government—seemed to be driven by progressive optimism as they tackled the problem with information programs, a drug czar, the language of war, and a new game plan.

The peak in May 1988 may be marked by the effect of Phase II of "Cocaine, The Big Lie," which was initiated in April 1988. The peak in March 1989 coincides with President Bush's appointment of William Bennett as the new drug czar, and the peak in September 1989 marks the attention given to Bush's television speech about his war on drugs, especially regarding Colombian drug lords, that generated significant media and public attention (Lichter & Lichter, 1990). Finally, the peak in January 1990 may relate to Bush's proclamation of success in his war (Shannon, 1990), though this is speculative. The history of the issue does not indicate a realization of an insurmountable obstacle for the sources of this coverage; rather, it is marked by a period of passionate enthusiasm by the government and the president to defeat the problem. For the media, the period offered a plethora of opportunities for issue and event coverage.

Decline Stage: February 1990–June 1991

The attention of the media—and the president and the public—shifted to matters of economics and the Persian Gulf beginning in early 1990 (Shannon, 1990). Many perceived the drug problem to be an issue of poor, inner-city residents and thus its importance shifted for the White majority who no longer saw the problem in its utterly destructive form (Barrett, 1990). Based on this conceptualization, the final phase of the media cycle (February 1990 to June 1991) appears to coincide with Downs' categorization of both decline and postproblem stages: The media's attention waned—as did that of the president and the public—but the objective indicators of the severity still remained. The entire stage has a mean frequency of stories of 98.

THE RELATIONSHIP OF CONTENT AND CYCLE

In addressing how the media structured interpretations and presentations of issue and event information during over time, the cyclic frequency structure of key issues and events is contrasted to the frequency structure of total media coverage for the respective stages of the cycle of coverage to determine if and how these key issues and events affected the structure of coverage for the respective stages. It should be noted that in the analysis various issues and events were used to determine the structure of the media coverage for the respective stages—in that the issues and events are not mutually exclusive, a crosstabulation of issues and events was run to determine any overlap. Two areas overlapped: sports/testing and violence/Colombia. In these cases, news reports about sports testing were counted as testing and violence in Colombia was counted as Colombia.

Preproblem Stage: July 1984–May 1986

The preproblem stage comprises 1,822 stories, accounting for 18% of the total media coverage in the study (see Table 4.2). The structure of this coverage can be explained by the issue of testing and the events of sports, Salazar, and deLorean, the sum of which accounts for 631 stories in the preproblem stage, or 35% of the coverage in the preproblem stage.

The coverage of John deLorean's drug trial accounts for the major media peak in August (see Fig. 4.7). The major peak in March 1985 appears to be driven by the extensive coverage of the kidnapping and murder of Enrique Camarena Salazar, the rise in coverage in September 1985 focuses on the drug arrest of baseball's Joe Pepitone, and the peak in March 1986 focuses heavily on President Reagan's push for drug testing of government employees and the drug-related problems of several sports heroes, including Keith Hernandez, Dale Berra, and Lawrence Taylor.

In many respects, the early phases of the preproblem stage strongly reflect Downs' (1972) definition of the preproblem stage—the problem exists, but it hasn't fully captured the media's attention. John deLorean's escapades almost appeared to be a scenario from a bad movie, the horrors of the Salazar incident were serious but foreign, and, the drug problems of Pepitone, and former pitcher Denny McLain, were a new item on the agenda of most sportswriters. However, as noted by NIDA (Adams et al., 1990) the drug problem was real. This reality was reflected in NIDA's information campaign in Spring 1986, and by President Reagan in his policy of testing. The major increase in sports-related drug problems in early 1986 also reflected an emerging problem that was beginning to arouse the attention of the media, the president, and the public.

Discovery Stage: June 1986–December 1987

The discovery stage involved 2,443 stories, accounting for 24% of the total media coverage in the study (see Table 4.2). The structure of the coverage can be explained using four key issues—testing, U.S. administration, international administration,

TABLE 4.2
Summary of the Media's Structuring of Issues and Events in the Four Stages of
the Drug Issue, 1984–1991

	Frequency in Stage	% of Total Media	% of Stage
Stage 1: Preproblem *July 1984–May 1986*	1822	18	35
Issues			
Testing	142		8
Events			
Sports	326		18
Salazar	92		5
deLorean	71		4
Stage 2: Discovery *June 1986–December 1987*	2443	24	31
Issues			
Testing	313		13
U.S. administration	157		6
International administration	122		5
Military	74		3
Events			
Len Bias	98		4
Stage 3: Plateau *January 1988–January 1990*	4129	41	28
Issues			
Violence	388		9
Events			
Columbia	405		10
Noriega	246		10
Bush's plan	49		1
War	49		1
Czar	25		1
Stage 4: Decline *February 1990–June 1991*	1668	17	32
Issues			
Violence	173		10
Events			
Barry	172		10
Columbia	92		6
Noriega	87		5
Czar	23		1

and military use—and the death of Len Bias, all of which accounted for 764 stories in this stage, or 31% of the stage's media coverage.

The major media activity of this period swings quickly off of the preproblem stage and mounts to a sharp peak from July through October of 1986 and then declines sharply for the rest of the stage (see Fig. 4.8). The thrust of the media's activity began with the June 1986 death of Len Bias, which captured the attention of the media and public and became a dramatic example of NIDA's call for public

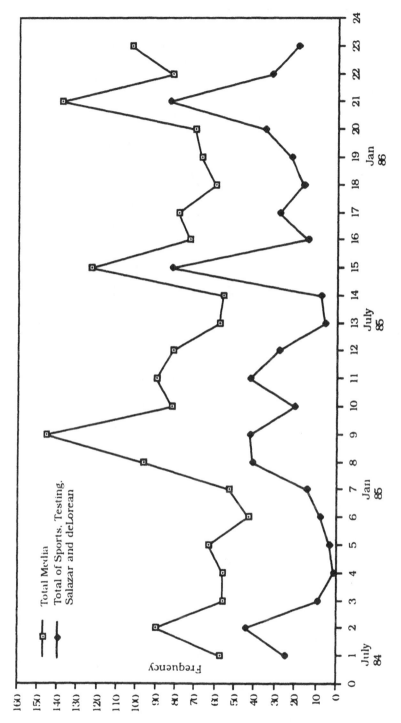

FIG. 4.7. Preproblem stage, July 1984–May 1986: Issue and event influences on media-content cycle.

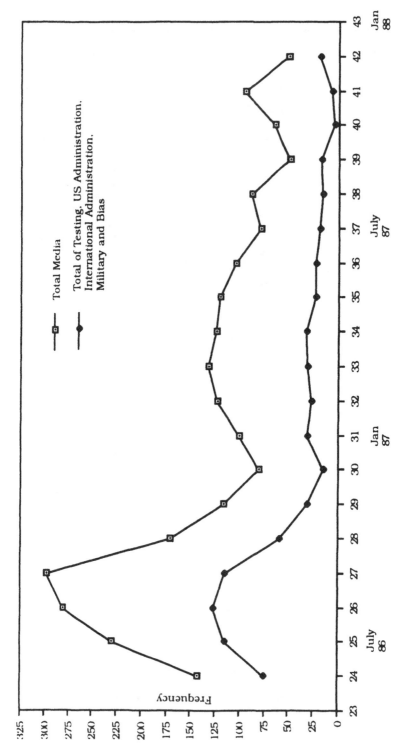

FIG. 4.8. Discovery stage, June 1986–December 1987: Issue and event influences on media-content cycle.

Frequency

Total Media

Total of Testing, US Administration.
International Administration.
Military and Bias

attention to the drug issue and President Reagan's program of testing and eventual war (Merriam, 1989). President Reagan's war on drugs is reflected in this early peak in the stage. His focus on the use of the military to stop the importation of drugs, his internal administrative efforts reflected in television addresses, and his turning to other nations to stop the influx of drugs into the United States are all made evident in this surge of media coverage. After his drug war seemed to die down at the end of 1986, media coverage remained around preproblem levels through most of the second half of the discovery stage. In all, the stage strongly reflects Downs' (1972) definition of the discovery stage as a period when there is a steep ascent of attention and transition from nonproblem to problem.

Plateau Stage: January 1988–January 1990.

In early 1988 media coverage began to increase. This marks the beginning of the plateau stage, which is made up of 4,129 stories about the drug issue and accounts for 41% of the media coverage of this study (see Table 4.2). The structure of the coverage is explained by the issues of violence and crime and five events: Colombia, Noriega, Bush's plan and war, and his drug czar. These issues and events accounted for 1172 stories, or 28% of the media coverage in the plateau stage. The media coverage in this stage is focused around three peaks: May 1988, March 1989, September 1989, and January 1990 (see Fig. 4.9).

The peak in May 1988 marks the reemergence of media interest in the issue. The content of this peak is explained mostly by heavy media coverage of the attempt to indict Manuel Noriega, which comprised nearly a quarter of the media coverage for the month. Media coverage decreased significantly until the next peak in March 1989. The content of this month is explained strongly by the issue of violence and crime, which comprises almost 25% of the media coverage of the month and reflects the serious implications of the spread of drugs, especially cocaine and crack. After a strong dip in coverage, media attention rose to its highest peak in September 1989. In August 1989, media coverage focused heavily on the drug-related events in Colombia, including a heavy focus on the activities of the drug lords, the Colombian government's efforts to stop the drug lords, the administrative relationship between the United States and Colombia, and the problems of crime and violence related to the spread of crack cocaine.

In September, President Bush attempted to assume a strong leadership role to stop drugs as he went before the American people declaring war on drugs and proposing his plan to control the drug problem. Media coverage in this month focused heavily on Colombia, Bush's plan, his language of war, and the use of the drug czar as the administrative head of the attack on drugs. As noted by Lichter and Lichter (1990), President Bush's efforts caused a rush of media activity—almost half of the media coverage of the issue appeared in September. Although coverage

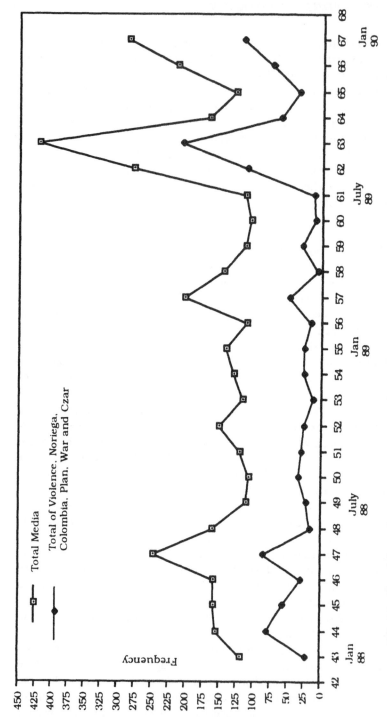

FIG. 4.9. The plateau stage, January 1988–January 1990: Issue and event influences on media-content cycle.

dropped sharply after September, the media continued coverage of Colombia, Noriega, and the problems of drug-related violence and crime. In the final peak in January 1990, the coverage focused more on President Bush's administrative actions and emerging claims of success in his war on drugs.

Decline Stage: February 1990–July 1991.

In February 1990, media coverage began a sharp drop, marking the beginning of the decline stage. This stage was made up of 1,668 stories about the drug issue and accounts for 17% of all media coverage in the study (see Table 4.2). The issue of violence and crime and the events of Washington, DC's Marion Barry, Colombia, Noriega, and the drug czar, all of which account for 32% of the media coverage in the stage, appear to explain the structure of the media's attention (see Fig. 4.10). Interestingly, the violence issue and the events about Colombia, Noriega, and the drug czar were also key indicators of the plateau stage; however, an examination of the media tone explains how they relate to the decline stage.

The struggle to capture Noriega ended in January 1990 when he surrendered and was indicted on drug trafficking. The focus of coverage changed from Noriega, the dictator beyond our reach, to Noriega, the prisoner who was "born again." The coverage of his imprisonment and trial continued in this stage, accounting for a quarter of the coverage of November 1990. In November the drug czar, William Bennett, then resigned amidst proclamations of success. Former Florida Governor Bob Martinez took up his role in March 1991, although he never sought nor attained the public spotlight that Bennett did.

Although problems continued in Colombia in 1990, 1991 marked a turning point as several key leaders of the Mendellin cartel, including Pablo Escobar Gaviria, surrendered to rather plush, custom-built prisons in June 1991. Finally, in the United States, Mayor Marion Barry was arrested in January 1990 and media coverage surrounding his indictment accounted for one third of the media coverage of the drug issue in June 1990. In some ways, the coverage of his ill-fated crack purchases presented a rather comic picture and, in line with Barrett's (1990) argument, may have made it out to be a "Black" issue. Against this backdrop, a study in February 1990 from the University of Michigan indicated that demand for drugs had decreased, and the government reported in May 1990 that the number of drug-related emergency-room admissions declined in the fourth quarter of 1989.

As noted by Downs (1972), although attention may decline in the final stages of the issue-attention cycle, the objective reality may be the same. NIDA figures indicate an upswing in cocaine-related emergency- room admissions in early 1991 (see Fig. 5.11). When the Mendellin cartel faced problems in Colombia, they were quickly replaced by the Cali cartel, and cocaine and crack were still a major problem for the United States.

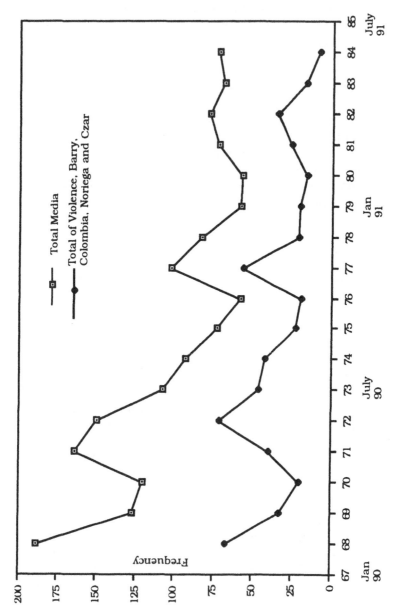

FIG. 4.10.   Decline stage, February 1990–June 1991: issue and event influences on media-content cycle.

CONCLUSION

In general, the relationship of cycle and content presents an interesting picture of how the structuring of the issues and events of the drug problem drove the issue through time. The cycle began in the preproblem stage with a movie-like event of an auto maker ruined in an attempt to sell drugs to fuel his ambition and the problems of numerous sports heroes caught in the web of drug use. For most people these were probably interesting, and possibly disheartening, events of a world beyond their environment. Next, the horrors of the drug cartels were brought home by the events surrounding a drug agent in Mexico. Again, however, for most people this was a rather distant and detached picture of an unreal world of corruption and intrigue. At the end of the stage, the reality of drugs was finally brought home by NIDA's information campaign and President Reagan's push for testing, which heralded the discovery stage.

The discovery stage was driven mainly by the political issues of drugs, as exemplified by President Reagan's war that focused heavily on testing, military use, and international conflict. However, amidst the backdrop of these issues, some abstract and some quite obtrusive, the media's spotlight focused on a healthy young American who, although on his way to fame and glory in the NBA, dropped dead in a college dorm room from a cocaine overdose. This personification of the reality of the drug problem was vivid and unavoidable for most Americans.

The plateau stage was primarily driven by political events. The president proclaimed a war; he had a plan; he had a czar; and he had a target—the drug lords of Colombia. Although this certainly captured the media and public's attention, the crest in the wave of media coverage was also driven by the sober reality of the issue of drug-related crime and violence.

The decline stage was again driven by drug events: Noriega was captured and imprisoned; the lords of drugs surrendered; and the spotlight focused on a politician who foolishly threatened his career with drugs—but again, against this backdrop, the issue of drug-related violence and crime continued. The media's attention waned; the president focused his attention elsewhere; and public concern decreased. The reality of the problem, however, was still on the streets and mounting again.

Chapter 5

Presidential Public Relations, Federal Expenditures, Real-World Cues, and Public Opinion

This chapter examines the second research question: How did the president structure interpretations and presentations of issue and event information over time? In addition, the chapter describes the trends in federal expenditures on the drug issue, real-world cue measures of the severity of the drug issue, and public opinion.

As with the media's structuring of issues and events, this analysis builds on the concept of information restructuring to determine if new presidential public relations interpretations and presentations were used by the president to keep his agenda of the drug issue alive, especially in the media's eye. This analysis examines and integrates three aspects of presidential public relations regarding the drug issue from 1984 to 1991 in order to determine if and how new information and the changing interpretations of the information about the issue of illegal drugs defined and drove the issue through time. First, presidential public relations activities, as presented in the Public Papers of the Presidents, are classified into issue and event categories. Second, the cycle of presidential public-relations activities, based on the monthly frequency of activities, is plotted and examined in relation to Downs' (1972) issue–attention cycle to determine if the cycle of activities in the study is represented by Downs' issue–attention model. Third, the frequency structure of key issues is contrasted against the frequency structure of total public-relations activities for the respective stages of the cycle of activities to determine if and how these key issues drove the structure of public-relations activities for the respective stages.

PRESIDENTIAL PUBLIC-RELATIONS CONTENT

As documented in the Public Papers of the Presidents from July 1984 to December 1988 (54 months), President Reagan engaged in 247 public relations activities, or 52% of the reported total for the period of the study. From January 1989 to June 1991 (30 months), President Bush engaged in 229 public relations activities, or 48% of the total for the period of the study; however, Bush engaged in almost the same amount of activities as Reagan in about half the time, thus indicating that Bush was almost twice as "PR-active" as Reagan concerning the drug issue.

The important issue for this analysis is the nature of the public-relations activities. To determine the drug issues and events, a content analysis was conducted of the 476 public-relations activities of the president for the period of the study as presented in the Public Papers of the Presidents. The content analysis evaluated the stories both in terms of their issue and event content. The issue categorization was based generally on a categorization of drug issues presented by Lichter and Lichter (1990). The event categorization was comprised from 98 unique events concerning the drug problem and based on Shaw's (1977) conceptualization of events.

ISSUES OF THE DRUG ISSUE

The content analysis of the issues of the drug problem is composed of 10 general issue categories, which subsume 28 specific issue categories. The 10 general issue categories are: use and demand (51 activities/11%), supply (6 activities/1%), enforcement/interest group activities (25 activities/5%), judicial activities (3 activities/1%), administrative activities (199 activities/42%), policy options (30 activities/6%), helping victims (125 activities/26%), public opinion and concern (1 activity/0.2%), political use of the drug issue (33 activities/7%), and miscellaneous (4 activities/1%).

Relative to the media, the president gave much heavier priority to: administrative activities (42% vs. 17% in the media), helping victims (26% vs. 9% in the media), and political use of the drug issue (7% vs. 1% in the media). Conversely, the media gave much heavier emphasis to the following than the president to: enforcement/interest group activities (22% vs. 5% for the president), judicial (16% vs. 1% for the president), and use and demand (19% vs. 11% for the president). In general, the president was more focused on the administrative, educational, and political aspects of the issue, which seems logical, whereas the media focused much more on the enforcement, judicial, and use and demand issues—each of which fit the front page and TV screen quite nicely. As in the media analysis in chapter 4, the major focus of the issue analysis in this chapter uses the 28 specific issue categories that are defined in Table 4.1.

The frequencies of the presidential issue activities for the 28 issue categories are presented in rank order in Fig. 5.1. Frequencies are used in the figure because of

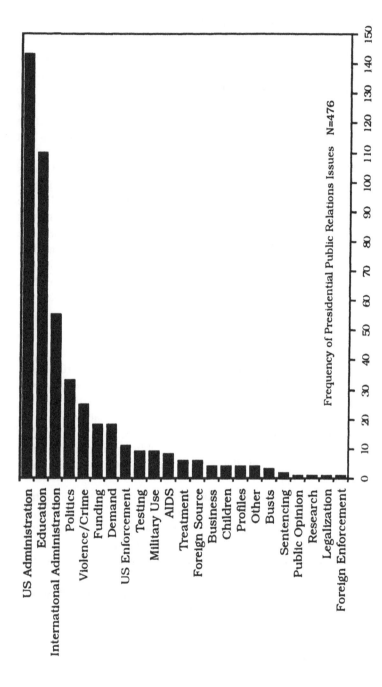

FIG. 5.1. Issue categories: Content analysis frequencies for presidential public-relations issues.

the small number of activities in many of the categories; however, the percentages, when meaningful, are noted in the discussion. The following issue categories accounted for 77% of the presidential public relations issues: U.S. administration (30%); education (23%); international administration (12%); political uses of the issue (7%); and violence and crime (5%).

A comparison of the issue frequencies (note that President Reagan's administration accounts for about twice as many months as that of President Bush in the study, i.e., a 2-to-1 ratio) for Presidents Reagan and Bush tends to suggest that Reagan placed a slightly stronger emphasis on demand, U.S. enforcement, testing, military use, AIDS, and foreign sources, whereas Bush placed a greater emphasis on U.S. administration, international administration, politics, and violence and crime. (See Fig. 5.2). Both presidents placed a great emphasis on education and prevention, which actually ranks relatively low on the media issue categorization.

EVENTS OF THE DRUG ISSUE

In the content analysis, 275 of the 476 presidential public relations activities were coded into specific event categories concerning discrete happenings related to drugs. As in the media content analysis, these event categories generally cross over into several issue categories. The presidential event content analysis used the same 98 event categories used in the media content analysis; in the analysis each of the categories that were used to label the 275 event-related activities is included in Fig. 5.3. Again, the frequency of events is used because of the small number of events in many of the categories and important percentages are noted when meaningful.

Unlike the members of the media, who tend to hone in on a specific issue and/or event in a story, both Reagan and Bush tended to use their public-relations opportunities to wander through a number of drug-related issues and events. As an example, Reagan went through a phase where no matter what he was talking or writing about, he would weave in a story about a heroin bust in California in which the couple who were arrested stashed their heroin in their young infant's diaper, attempting to conceal the drugs from the police. However, the major focus of the public relations activity was usually easy to categorize.

Seven events account for almost 70% of the event-related activities of the president: public-relations activities (27%), such as proclamations about National Drug Abuse Education Week and "Just Say No To Drugs" Week; President Bush's plan to combat drugs (12%); announcements concerning appointments to key drug-related government positions (8%); executive action (6%), such as executive orders about a drug-free workplace in the Federal government; Congress (6%), which typically included a presidential speaking engagement to raise funds for a member of Congress that included a speech on drug abuse; Reagan's plan to combat drugs (5%); and Bush's Points of Light program, which was designed to spearhead community and voluntary actions to stop drug abuse.

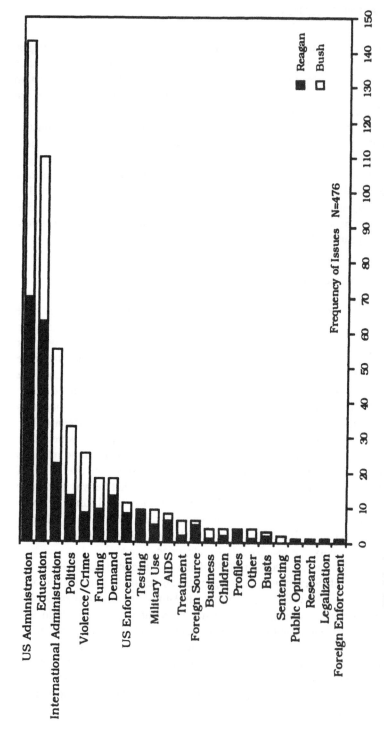

FIG. 5.2. Issue categories: Frequency of public-relations issues for the Reagan and Bush administrations.

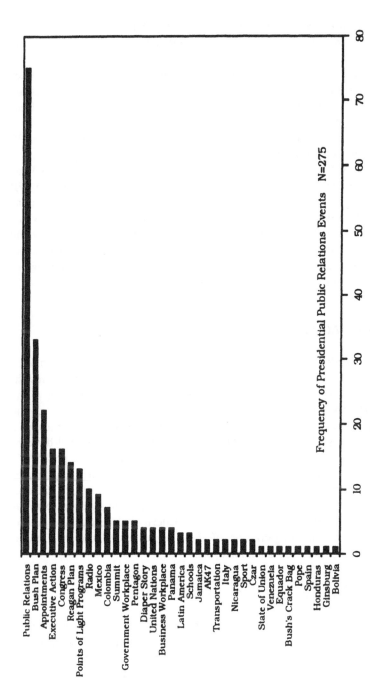

FIG. 5.3. Event categories: Content analysis frequencies for presidential public-relations events.

A comparison of the events focused on in the public-relations activities by Presidents Reagan and Bush suggests some major differences in public-relations style. Again, due to large number of event categories with few elements, Fig. 5.4 exhibits the frequency, and not the percentage, of events per category. When making comparisons across the Reagan and Bush administrations, one must remember that the Reagan term represents 54 months in the study, whereas the Bush term represents only 30.

Without question, Reagan had a much stronger penchant for drug-related PR events, such as Crack/Cocaine Awareness Month, National Family Week, and Child Health Day. Bush attempted to "sell" his plan of attack on drugs, led by Drug Czar William Bennett; Reagan, on the other hand, had less than half as many PR activities related to his plan of attack. Finally, Bush tried to sway the American public to community and voluntary action with his Points of Light program, which slightly outnumbered Reagan's attempts to preach drug prevention with his radio "fireside" chats. Other than these major event activities, most of the other event categories have relatively low frequencies and suggest the rather wide range of events related to this complex and diverse issue.

THE CYCLE OF ACTIVITIES

As noted in the media content analysis in chapter 4, when media coverage is plotted over time the result is usually a recurring (and sometimes exponential in growth) cycle, with each cycle, or portion of the cycle, representing a restructuring of the issue via issue and event information (Rogers et al., 1991). A similar cyclic restructuring occurs for the cycle of presidential public relations activities; in a similar light, Downs' (1972) concept of the issue–attention cycle, although directed at the effects of information on the public, can also be applied to the president's perception of a problem in that the president is a public figure with a highly focused sense of attention to problems and a command of the media's spotlight (Behr & Iyengar, 1985; Gilbert, 1981). In this section, the president's public relations activities are examined to determine the cyclical pattern of his restructuring of the issue and the possible categorization of these cycles in relation to Downs' conceptualization of the issue–attention cycle.

Preproblem Stage: July 1984–May 1986

In the period from July 1984 to May 1986, presidential public relations activity fluctuated mildly around an average 2.56 activities per month (see Fig. 5.5). This appears to equate to Down's categorization of the preproblem stage of an issue, in which a problem exists, as indicated by the introduction of crack cocaine (Johnston, 1989) but has not captured the public's (in this case the president's) attention. However, the drug issue was not exactly at this stage around the Reagan White

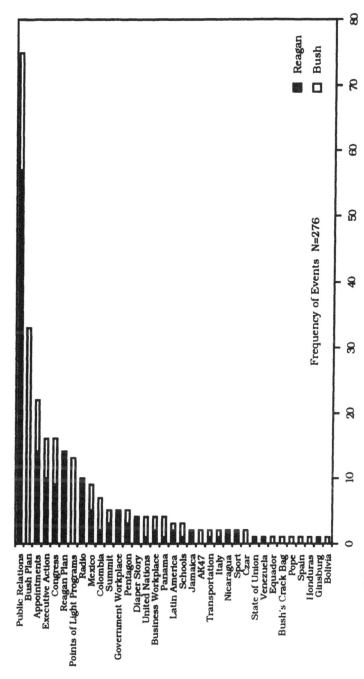

FIG. 5.4. Event categories: Frequency of public-relations events for Reagan and Bush administrations.

63

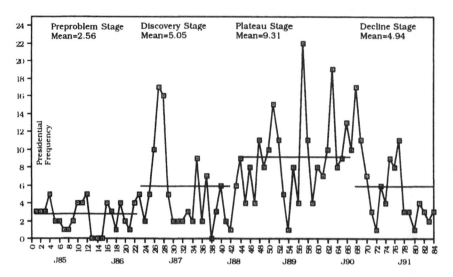

FIG. 5.5. Frequencies and means of the four stages of the presidential public relations cycle: July 1984–June 1991.

House. NIDA's "Just Say No" campaign was formally organized in 1984 and launched in 1985 with the help of Nancy Reagan, whose public image greatly benefited from the campaign (see chapter 1, this volume.) However, in terms of President Reagan the issue was just beginning to take hold.

Discovery Stage: June 1986–December 1987

Beginning in June 1986, President Reagan seemed to catch his wife's "antidrug" passion. In August, the frequency of presidential public-relations activity increased to 10, and then shot up to 17 in September. In October it dipped slightly to 16. After this peak, the frequency of coverage declined to preproblem-stage levels until May and July of 1987, when it peaked mildly to 7 and 9 activities per month respectively. After July 1987 it again dipped to pre-problem stage levels. The June-to-October interest was driven by strong public information campaigns by NIDA ("Cocaine, The Big Lie") that began in April, political interests in the 1986 election, Len Bias' death in June, and Reagan's war on drugs, which he emphasized between August and October of 1986 (Merriam, 1989). Reagan's flurry of activity then all but died out in the second half of 1986; however, the period from June 1986 to December 1987 averaged 5.05 activities per month, a marked increase compared to the preproblem period, and this second phase of public relations activity suggested a discovery stage for the president in which there was a sudden, steep ascent of attention and transition from low to high priority.

Plateau Stage: January 1988–January 1990

The period from January 1988 to January 1990 has a monthly mean frequency of public-relations activities of 9.31 and is marked by five sharp peaks in presidential activity (the last is actually in the first month of the decline stage), four of which appear to relate to heightened media coverage during the period. The first peak in presidential activity in June 1988 was made up of 11 activities and follows the first peak in heightened media attention during the discovery stage in May 1988, when the media presented 247 stories. The second peak occurred in September 1988 and contained 15 activities; however, this does not seem to relate strongly to the media agenda. The third, in March 1989, included 22 activities—the highest monthly frequency of presidential activity in the study. This peak relates to the second in media coverage during this stage of 201 stories. The fourth peak, which occurred during September 1989 indicated that there were 19 public-relations activities. This month represented the pinnacle of media attention in the study with 419 stories. Finally, in February 1990, which is actually the first month of the decline stage, the president engaged in 17 public-relations activities. This is noted because it follows the fourth peak in media attention in January 1990, the last month of the discovery stage, when the media presented 285 stories.

As did the media, the President seemed to be in a cyclic frenzy of activity during this stage, although he seemed to be acting in unison or following the media rather than leading. In addition, the President and the government seemed to be driven by progressive optimism as they tackled the problem with information programs, a drug czar, the language of war, and a new game plan.

Phase II of "Cocaine, The Big Lie," which was initiated in April 1988, was followed by heightened media attention in May and heightened presidential attention in June. The presidential and media peaks in March 1989 coincided with Bush's appointment of Bennett as the new drug czar and the presidential and media peaks in September 1989 corresponded with Bush's television speech about his war on drugs, especially regarding Colombian drug lords, that generated significant media and public attention (Lichter & Lichter, 1990). Finally, the media peak in January 1990 seemed to relate to Bush's proclamation of success in his war (Shannon, 1990), which Bush followed in February 1990 with numerous public relations activities about Colombia and his Points of Light program. This may have been his way of distancing his administration from the problem and turning the issue back into the hands of local communities and voluntarism—much in the way it began with Reagan.

Decline Stage: February 1990–June 1991

Following President Bush's Points of Light and Colombia focus in February 1990, his attention, like that of the media and the public, shifted to matters of economics and the Persian Gulf until November 1990, when William Bennett resigned. The peak of presidential activity in this stage centered around Bennett's resignation and included 11 activities. After this peak, the level of presidential activity declined sharply to a monthly mean of 4.94. The final phase of the presidential cycle (February 1990 to June 1991), like that of the media, appears to coincide with Downs' categorization of both decline and postproblem phases: The president's attention waned as he declared success on the war on drugs. Yet even as he heralded victory, the real-world indicators concerning the severity of the problem steadily rose (see Fig. 5.11).

THE RELATIONSHIP OF CONTENT AND CYCLE

To determine how the president structured interpretations and presentations of issue information over time, the frequency structure of key drug-related issues was contrasted to the total frequency structure of presidential public relations activity for the respective stages of the study. As in the media analysis, this analysis seeks to descriptively plot the frequency of presidential activity for the key issues in the respective stages of the issue with the total frequency of presidential public-relations activity. However, unlike the media analysis, the analysis of presidential public-relations activity does not include any of the event categories, which are not mutually exclusive relative to the issue categories. Only key issues are used because, unlike the media analysis, the key event categories are highly correlated with the key issue categories. As an example, the activities concerning the event category of Bush's Points of Light program were virtually all subsumed within the issue category of education/prevention. Therefore, the analysis only includes the key issues; however, where appropriate, the analysis discusses the key events that are subsumed in the key issues of the analysis.

Preproblem Stage: July 1984–May 1986

The preproblem stage includes a total of 59 public relations activities, accounting for 12% of the total presidential public relations activity (See Table 5.1). The structure of this coverage can be explained by using the issues of education/prevention, U.S. administration, international administration, military use, and U.S. enforcement, the sum of which accounts for 52 public relations activities in the preproblem stage, or 88% of the activities in the stage.

Although the media focused heavily on sports, testing, Salazar, and deLorean during the preproblem stage, President Reagan's major thrust of education/prevention seemed to relate more closely to Nancy Reagan's antidrug education crusade. Thirty of the 52 public relations activities used to describe the structure of this stage

TABLE 5.1
Summary of the Presidents' Structuring of Issues in the Four Stages
of the Drug Issue, 1984–1991

	Frequency in Stage	% of Total PR	% of Stage
Stage 1: Preproblem *June 1984–May 1986*	59	12	88
Issues			
Education/prevention	30		51
U.S. administration	11		19
International administration	7		12
Military	2		3
U.S. enforcement	2		3
Stage 2: Discovery *June 1986–December 1987*	96	21	74
Issues			
U.S. administration	32		33
Education/prevention	21		22
Testing	7		7
International administration	7		7
Demand	4		4
Stage 3: Plateau *January 1988–January 1990*	242	49	81
Issues			
U.S. administration	84		35
Education/prevention	39		16
International administration	30		12
Violence	14		6
Demand	12		5
Funding	9		4
AIDS	7		3
Stage 4: Decline *February 1990–June 1991*	79	17	90
Issues			
Education/prevention	19		24
U.S. administration	15		19
Political uses	14		18
International administration	11		14
Violence	7		9
Funding	5		6

concern education and prevention. For example, in September 1984 President Reagan called on the American people to combat drugs through abuse education, community involvement, and voluntarism, and in October 1984 he heralded the efforts of D.C. Comics to teach children about drug abuse through their comic books. However, 11 of the 52 activities concerned U.S. administration of the drug issue. Reagan presented his administrative strategy on September 27, 1984, in the 1984 National Strategy for the Prevention of Drug Abuse and Drug Trafficking, which included a focus on prevention of drug abuse through awareness and action, drug law enforcement, international cooperation to eliminate the production and trafficking of illegal drugs, and health-related treatment and research activities.

President Reagan's strategy concerning international cooperation was also related to the efforts of his wife during this period, and the issue accounted for seven public-relations activities during the this stage. On October 19, 1985, Nancy Reagan opened the door to international cooperation as she met with 31 other first ladies at the United Nations to develop a cooperative program to stop drug abuse. This effort culminated in a trip by President and Nancy Reagan in May 1986, the last month of this stage, to Malaysia, Thailand, Guam, and Hawaii to help establish cooperative programs concerning drugs.

President Reagan's strategy concerning U.S. enforcement and his focus on using the military to stop drug importation each accounted for two activities in this stage. The tone of this strategy was best exemplified by a radio address on October 6, 1984, in which the president told the American public of his plans to use the military to stop drug importation and to develop 13 new organized-crime and drug-enforcement task forces under the control of Vice President George Bush and Attorney General Edwin Meese, to assist in foreign countries' efforts to control production and state efforts to eradicate drug production.

In general, Reagan's public-relations activities, although at a relatively low level during this stage, tend to suggest that the President and Nancy Reagan were slightly ahead of the curve concerning their appreciation of the problematic nature of drugs. Although the President and his wife focused heavily on education and voluntarism to solve the problem in this stage, their efforts also suggest that they were beginning to expand the scope of the problem to the international and enforcement arenas, especially in the latter part of this preproblem stage. This focus on eradication and education is exemplified by his "America's Agenda for the Future" message to Congress on February 6, 1986, in which he called on Congress to continue their efforts to eradicate illegal drugs before they can be harvested and to reduce the demand for these narcotics by opening the eyes of America's young people.

Discovery Stage: June 1986–December 1987

The discovery stage includes a total of 96 public relations activities, accounting for 21% of the entire study's public relations activities (see Table 5.1). The structure of public relations activity can be explained by the five key issues of U.S. administration, education/prevention, testing, international administration, and demand, all of which accounted for 71 activities in this stage, or 74% of the stage's public-relations activities (see Fig. 5.6). The president's priorities during this stage roughly matched the media's issue agenda of testing, U.S. administration, and international administration, though not in that order. The media tended to highlight the issue of testing much more heavily, and they also focused on the use of the

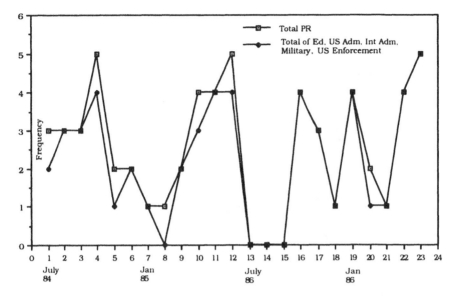

FIG. 5.6. Preproblem stage, July 1984–May 1986: Issue influences on presidential public-relations cycle.

military and Len Bias' death, which Reagan only addressed as a secondary focus in his efforts.

Thirty-two of the 71 public relations activities, or 33% of the activities in the stage, concern U.S. administration, whereas 21%, or 22%, concern education/prevention. Compared to the preproblem stage, President Reagan seemed to switch his major emphasis from education and prevention to a more active focus on the efforts of the administration to tackle the drug problem; that is, his war on drugs. In addition, the presidential agenda in this stage included 7 activities concerning drug testing, 7 concerning international administration, and 4 concerning the issue of demand. As suggested in Fig. 5.7, the major thrust of activity in this stage occurred between August and October of 1986.

President Reagan's focus on U.S. administration began on August 4, 1986, with the release of information about his National Campaign Against Drug Abuse, in which he established six major goals that he hoped would be the final stage of a national strategy to eradicate drug abuse. On September 4, 1986, President and Nancy Reagan presented these goals to the American people in their first joint national press conference: (a) stop drug use in the workplace; (b) stop drug use by the youth of America; (c) tackle health dangers stemming from drug abuse, including research in treatment, prevention, and testing methods; (d) enhance international cooperation to eradicate drugs; (e) crack down on drug pushers through enforcement; and (f) increase public awareness of the dangers of illegal drugs through efforts of both the public and private sectors.

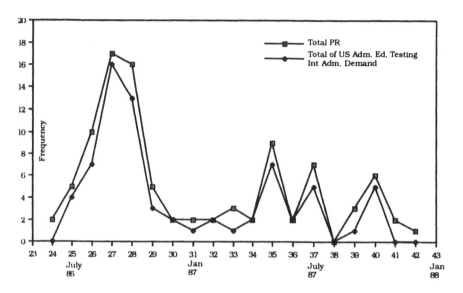

FIG. 5.7.   Discovery stage, June 1986–December 1987: Issue influences on presidential public-relations cycle.

On September 14, President Reagan reemphasized these six goals in a national television address about his National Campaign Against Drug Abuse. He followed this PR effort with the signing of the Drug-Free America Act of 1986 on September 15, which operationalized his six goals, and the issuing on September 15 of the Drug-Free Workplace Executive Order, which delineated the roles of various federal departments to reduce workplace drug use, including testing of transportation system workers and reducing illegal drug activity in federal public housing units.

President Reagan also focused on the issues of education, demand, and testing during August to October of 1986, generally as spin-offs of his goals for his war on drugs. As an example, all public-relations activities concerning drug testing of federal workers happened in this August-to-October period. Conversely, his efforts concerning international administration tended to occur more heavily in the latter part of the discovery stage from May 1987 through October 1987. As an example, he focused heavily on the international administration issue of the International Conference on Drug Abuse and Illicit Trafficking held in Vienna, Austria, in June 1987.

The Plateau Stage: January 1988–January 1990

The plateau stage comprises a total of 242 public relations activities, accounting for 49% of the entire study's public relations activities (see Table 5.1). The structure of public relations activity can be explained using seven key issues: U.S.

administration, education/prevention, international administration, violence/crime, demand, funding, and AIDS. These seven issues accounted for 195 activities in this stage, or 81% of the stage's public-relations activities. The presidents' priorities (note that Bush entered office in January 1989) during this stage roughly matched the media's agenda of violence/crime, Noriega, Colombia, Bush's plan, Bush's war on drugs, and the drug czar; however, the media tended to focus more heavily on the event aspects of the drug issue, whereas the presidents, to a degree, tended to deal with the drug problem in a broader, issue format. The number of important issues in this stage tends to reflect Downs' (1972) definition of the plateau stage as one in which there is a realization that the problem is not easy to solve and that it is quite complex; however, around the White House the tone was one of solving and winning the problem and not of surrendering to its problematic and complex nature.

President Reagan began the plateau stage with a heavy focus on the issue of demand, which accounted for 12 public-relations activities during the plateau stage, or 5% of the public-relations activities during this stage. The early months of the plateau stage also included a focus on international administration, especially in relation to positive aspects of the United State's relationship with Mexico and negative aspects of Nicaragua and its leader Manuel Noriega. The issue of international administration accounted for 30 public-relations activities, or 12% of the activities in the plateau stage. Also in June 1988, the first mild peak in presidential activity of the plateau stage, President Reagan addressed the issue of AIDS and drugs. In August 1988 he then focused heavily on this issue, which accounted for 7 public-relations activities or 3% of the activities in the plateau stage.

The second major peak of presidential activity occurred in September 1988 and focused heavily on the issues of U.S. administration, education/prevention, and funding of the U.S. drug programs. During the plateau stage, U.S. administration accounted for 84 public-relations activities, or 35% of the activities in the plateau stage; education/prevention accounted for 39 activities, or 16% of the activities in this stage; and funding accounted for 9 activities, or 4% of the activities in this stage. As an example of the focus on these three issues, on September 23 President Reagan issued a statement on the Omnibus Drug Initiative of 1988 in which he noted that the House bill contained provisions that would substantially strengthen the United States' ability to detect, try, and punish those who were engaged in drug trafficking and related criminal activity. In addition, he also focused on his efforts to secure additional funding for his efforts to combat drugs and educate the youth of America about drug abuse.

After September 1988, presidential interest declined sharply as the nation prepared for the November 1988 presidential election (see Fig. 5.8). After the election Bush emerged in March 1989 with a flurry of activity concerning the drug issue—the highest amount in the entire presidential agenda of the study. On January 27, 1989, Bush named William Bennett as director of National Drug Control Policy and began to use the term "drug czar." On February 9, Bush requested an additional

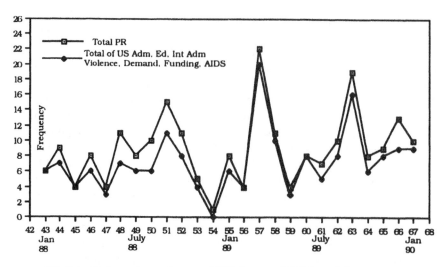

FIG. 5.8. Plateau stage, January 1988–January 1990: Issue influences on presidential public-relations cycle.

$1 billion from Congress to help fight drugs, and in March began to preach his war on drugs and the abilities of Bennett. At Bennett's swearing in on March 13, President Bush announced that his war on drugs comprised four components: education, treatment, interdiction and enforcement.

Following Bennett's placement in office, he and Bush held numerous meetings with law enforcement groups, students, and special interest groups to sell the president's plan. Bush also began to address the drug-related issue of violence and crime, which accounted for 14 public-relations activities, or 6% of the activities in the plateau stage. Focus on the issue of violence and crime began in March 1989 with Bennett's efforts to ban the AK-47 rifle in order to reduce drug-related violence among gangs. On June 15, President Bush sent a message to Congress concerning the Comprehensive Violent Crime Control Act of 1989, in which he tied the surge in violent crime in the United States to illegal drugs and proposed numerous steps to reduce violent drug crimes, including drug testing of prisoners as a condition of release from prison. President Bush also addressed the issue of violence in regard to drug-related crimes in Latin America, such as the assassination of Colombian President Luis Carlos Galan in August 1989.

After President Bush's flurry of activity in March 1989, his public-relations efforts were relatively mild until September 1989 when he addressed the nation about his National Drug Control Strategy with a bag of crack in his hand. His public relations efforts in September were second only to his efforts in March 1989 in terms of the frequency of events. In his address to the nation, President Bush again focused on his four-point strategy of education, treatment, interdiction, and enforcement, and he specifically addressed the problems of violence and drug production in Colombia. At the time of this event, public attention had grown to its highest level, as had media attention. After September, President Bush's public-relations efforts declined sharply, as did media and public interest, until the end of the plateau stage in January 1990 with the exception of a little flurry of educational activity in December 1989.

Decline Stage: February 1990–July 1991

The decline stage comprises a total of 79 public relations activities, accounting for 17% of the entire study's public relations activities (see Table 5.1). The structure of public-relations activity can be explained by six key issues: education/prevention, U.S. administration, political use of the drug issue, international administration, violence, and funding. These six issue accounted for 71 activities in this stage, or 90% of the stage's public relations activities. As in the plateau stage, President Bush's priorities during the decline stage roughly matched the media's agenda of violence, Colombia, Noriega, and the drug czar, but again the media tended to focus more heavily on the event aspects of the drug issue, whereas President Bush tended to deal with the problem in a broader, issue format. Although Downs (1972) defined the decline/postproblem stages as being driven by inattention and frustration whereas the objective reality of the problem is unchanged, the presidential tone was again driven by optimism as the real-world measures of the severity of the problem dipped slightly and offered some hope for success. Although the dip was temporary, Bush seemed content to announce victory and move on to other agenda items, possibly suggesting his frustration and ensuing inattention to what seemed to be a no-win situation.

The first month of the decline stage (February 1990) was actually one of the most PR-active months of the study for the president (see Fig. 5.9). This flurry of activity comprised a heavy focus on the signing of the United Nation's Convention Against Illegal Traffic in Narcotic Drugs and Psychotropic Substances; the Drug Summit in Cartagena, Colombia, and the resulting Declaration of Cartagena; and the Bolivia–U.S. Essential Chemicals Agreement. These activities largely accounted for the stage's focus on the issue of international administration, which comprised 11 public relations activities, or 9% of the activities in the decline stage. President Bush's efforts concerning his Points of Light recognition program also accounted for the sharp peak in February and much of the activity in March 1990.

The level of presidential public-relations activity declined steadily until the fall of 1990, when President Bush hit the 1990 campaign trail for Republican hopefuls. Much of the increased public-relations activity in September and October concerned the issue of political uses of the drug issue, in which Bush used speaking opportunities for candidates to talk about the drug issue and the success of his plan and czar. However, on November 8, 1990, he accepted the letter of resignation of William Bennett as director of National Drug Control Policy, and on November 30 nominated Florida Governor Bob Martinez as his replacement. As with the media,

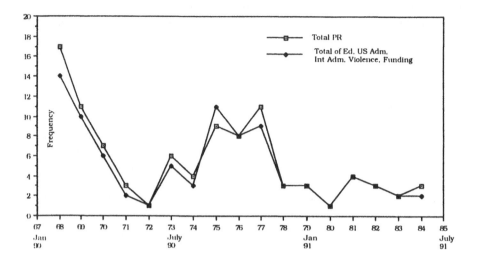

FIG. 5.9. Decline stage, February 1990–June 1991: Issue influences on presidential public-relations cycle.

the heavy focus of the presidential public-relations activities in November concerned this administrative issue.

Following this flurry of activity in November, the drug issue fell from the presidential public relations agenda as President Bush claimed victory over the drug problem and pointed to government statistics that suggested decreases in monthly cocaine use, drug-related emergencies, and addictive drug use. Although his statistical readings were correct, the decline was temporary—the severity of the problem reemerged; the president's attention did not.

FEDERAL EXPENDITURES, REAL-WORLD CUES, AND PUBLIC OPINION

This final section descriptively examines the trend in the final three agendas of the study. Although this study is not an examination of the economics of the drug issue nor a detailed analysis of the medical aspects of the issue, the trends in federal expenditures and cocaine-related emergency-room admissions do offer interesting insights into the issue's policy and real-world ramifications, and, as noted previously, both of these measures serve as important control variables in the following multivariate analyses of agendas. Conversely, the analysis of the trend in public opinion reflects the world of perception, much like that of the media and presidential agendas, and offers important insights into the development of public consensus about the issue.

Federal Expenditures

The media and presidential public-relations agendas reflect a roller coaster ride of vacillating perceptions of importance that generally rose, peaked, and declined (see Fig. 5.10). The government's policy agenda, as measured by total federal expenditures in 1967 constant dollars rose steadily, but unlike the media and presidential measures, it never dipped in time. Although the use of constant dollars is important to control for effects in inflation and the changing value of the dollar, and for the following multivariate analyses, administrators' budgets typically focus on percentage change relative to the previous year. Therefore, Table 5.2 presents a summary of the federal budgets in real dollars, as based on the 1991 National Drug Control Strategy Budget Summary, and delineates the percentage change from year to year. In addition, the table includes the federal budgets for 1983 and 1992, which are not included in the constant dollar analysis in Fig. 5.10, to offer some idea of the dollar amounts and annual change immediately prior to and following the period of the study.

In 1983, the year prior to the beginning of this study, the federal government spent $1.88 billion on the drug problem; however, this budget increased by 25% in 1984 to $2.34 billion. The remaining federal budgets (1985 and 1986) in the preproblem stage increased only 11% and 5% respectively, tending to confirm the preproblem status of this period.

The 1987 federal budget, which is the key budget in the discovery stage (June 1986–December 1987), reflects the greatest annual increase of any of the budgets in the study with a 70% increase compared to 1986. This dramatic change tends to

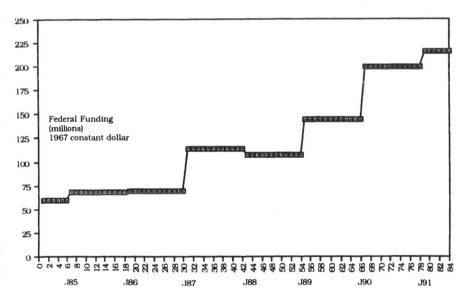

FIG. 5.10. Policy agenda: federal expenditures on the drug problem.

TABLE 5.2
Summary of Annual Federal Expenditures in Real Dollars

Year	President	Real Dollars (Billions)	% Change
1983	Reagan	1.88	
1984	Reagan	2.34	+25%
1985	Reagan	2.60	+11%
1986	Reagan	2.74	+5%
1987	Reagan	4.65	+70%
1988	Reagan	4.56	-2%
1989	Bush	6.40	+40%
1990	Bush	9.38	+47%
1991	Bush	10.52	+12%
1992	Bush	11.65	+11%

reflect the definition of the discovery stage as a period in which there is a sudden steep ascent of attention and transition from nonproblem to problem status.

The 1988 budget, which started at the beginning of the plateau stage (January 1988–January 1990), was the only budget in the study that decreased (-2%) relative to the previous year. Although the decrease was minimal, the annual budget was still high relative to the budgets in the preproblem stage. In 1988, President Reagan engaged in heightened public-relations activity, especially in the months from June to September of that year; however, his efforts to increase the budget actually declined.

President Bush entered office in January 1989 in the middle of the plateau stage (January 1988–January 1990). In February 1989, he requested and received an almost $1 billion dollar increase in the federal budget for that year, primarily to assist with his war of interdiction and enforcement. This increased federal outlay is reflected in the 40% increase in the budget relative to 1988. In many ways this tends to reflect the definition of the plateau stage as a period of realization that the problem is not easy to solve and that it is quite complex. Although President Bush tackled the issue during this year with the optimism of his drug czar and his war on drugs, he also realized the need to put dollars behind his actions to deal with this complex, multifaceted issue. The 1990 budget, which began in the last month of the plateau stage, increased significantly relative to the 1989 budget and again reflected the administration's efforts to cope with this complex problem.

After President Bush's high amount of public-relations activity in February 1990, the first month of the decline stage (February 1990–June 1991), his interest declined until the autumn of 1990 when he started his reelection campaign and dealt with the resignation of William Bennett. This decline in interest seems to parallel the mild 12% increase in the 1991 budget. In addition, the federal 1992 budget (not included in the analysis) again reflected a mild increase (11%) in federal expenditures and tended to reflect the dwindling interest of the issue reflected in the media, presidential, and public-opinion agendas.

Real-World Cue: Cocaine-Related Emergency-Room Admissions

The reality measure of the drug problem was a bit more steady in its course (see Fig. 5.11). Unlike the fickle media and presidents, who scamper about the amusement park of public issues, reality climbed steadily, devoid of the attraction of other rides, until the second half of 1989, when it declined briefly until the beginning of 1991. The severity of the problem then steadily climbed.

The frequency of cocaine-related emergency-room admissions in the pre-problem stage (July 1984–May 1986) tends to confirm the categorization of this period as a preproblem. The level of admissions was constant and relatively low. Beginning in the discovery stage (June 1986–December 1987), the frequency of admissions increased dramatically and continued to rise until the autumn of 1989 when it declined for a period of 15 months. In January 1991 it then again began to rise steadily. The decline in late 1989 and 1990 tends to support the categorization of this period as the decline stage and offers some support to President Bush's proclamations of victory in the war on drugs; however, the increasing trend in 1991 counters this categorization. The drug problem increased and the number of people who suffered rose with only a slight dip on a ride that seemed to never end. Although the reality of the problem continued, the other agenda players got off the ride.

Public Opinion

The aggregate measure of the public's opinion of drugs as the most important problem in the country also took a roller coaster ride, but unlike the media and

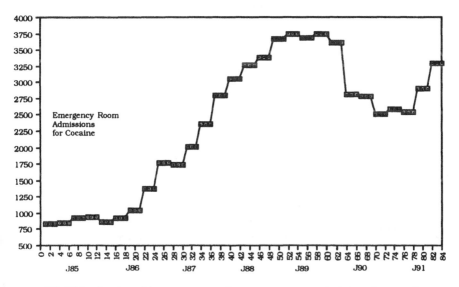

FIG. 5.11.   Real-world cue measure: Emergency room admissions for cocaine.

presidential agendas it did not take quite as many dips and turns (see Fig. 5.12). In many ways, public opinion was much more like the real-world cue trend as it built up to peak, declined, and then mildly increased at the end of the study in unison with the real-world cue.

In the preproblem stage (July 1984–May 1986), public concern about drugs as the country's most important problem was below 5%. In the discovery stage (June 1986–December 1987), public concern began to rise, especially around July and August of 1986, when attention focused on the death of Len Bias and President Reagan's war on drugs. Public concern for drugs as the most important problem hovered around 10% until the plateau stage (January 1988–January 1990), when public concern began to rise steadily until it reached a peak of 66% in September 1989. At this time, Bush addressed the nation about drugs on television and aroused both media and public attention; however, this attention waned quickly, and public concern decreased steadily in the decline stage (February 1990–June 1991) until it bottomed out in January 1991. From February 1991 to June 1991 it sparked mildly to the 10% range, much like the final rise in the real-world cue measure.

CONCLUSION

The analysis of the media agenda in chapter 4 suggests a steadily rising roller coaster ride of media attention, driven by key issues and events, that plummeted in the early part of 1991. The cycle of coverage seems to coincide with Downs' issue–attention model, which comprises the preproblem, discovery, plateau, and decline stages.

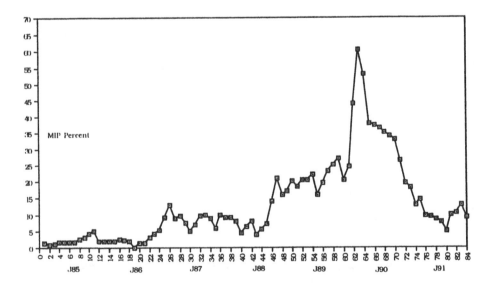

FIG. 5.12. Public opinion of drugs as the most important problem.

The analysis of presidential public-relations efforts in this chapter also suggests a roller coaster ride through time, although the presidents' roller coaster took a few more severe dips and turns.

During the preproblem stage (July 1984–May 1986), Reagan spoke out about drugs less than three times a month. In the early part of the stage his interest was rising especially in terms of education and prevention; in the latter part of the stage his war plan began to emerge. At the beginning of the discovery stage (June 1986–December 1987), President Reagan dramatically increased his efforts concerning drugs as he mounted his war on drugs in the summer of 1986. During the balance of the discovery stage, his efforts fluctuated. During the election campaign of 1988, presidential attention rose and declined sharply after the November 1988 election. President Bush's efforts rose dramatically under the guidance of William Bennett, who made drugs Bush's number one priority. However, after the televised speech in September 1989, Bush's efforts steadily declined, much like the attention of the media.

The government's policy agenda, as measured by total federal expenditures, rose steadily; however, unlike the media and presidential measures, it never dipped in time although the percentage change in annual budgets declined toward the end of the study's time frame. The budgets and annual percentage change in budgets in the preproblem stage were relatively low. The 1987 federal budget, which is the key budget in the discovery stage, reflected the greatest annual increase of any of the budgets in the study with a 70% increase compared to 1986. This dramatic change tends to reflect the definition of the discovery stage as a period in which there is a sudden steep ascent of attention and transition from nonproblem to problem status. At the beginning of the plateau stage, the 1988 budget actually decreased; after President Bush entered office in January 1989, however, the 1989 and 1990 budgets grew steadily until the 1991 and 1992 budgets, which reflected minor percentage increases, possibly confirming the minimalization of presidential and federal enthusiasm for a hard-to-win issue.

Although constant during the preproblem stage, the real-world cue measure of emergency-room admissions for cocaine-related injury rose steadily in the discovery stage, peaked in the latter part of the plateau stage, dropped sharply in the latter part of the plateau stage, and then rose in the final part of the decline stage. The decline in late 1989 and 1990 tends to support the categorization of this period as the decline stage and offers some support to President Bush's proclamations of victory in war on drugs; however, the increasing trend in 1991 suggested the continuing horrors that the issue had to offer.

The aggregate measure of the public's opinion of drugs as the country's most important problem also took a roller coaster ride, but unlike the media and presidential agendas it did not take quite as many dips and turns. In many ways, public opinion was much more like the real-world cue trend as it built to a peak, declined, and then mildly increased at the end of the study.

Chapter 6

ARIMA Modeling and Analysis of the Drug Issue Agendas

This chapter examines the third and fourth research questions: What were the interactions of the drug-issue agendas of the president, the media, and the public, while controlling for the policy agenda and a real-world measure of the severity of the drug problem; and how did the relationships of these agendas differ during the Reagan and Bush presidencies?

In essence, this analysis attempts to determine which of the agendas drove the other agendas over time. Was the media driving the issue (Kerr, 1986)? Was the issue driven by the presidents (Barrett, 1990; Shannon, 1990)? Was the reality of the problem driving public attention (MacKuen, 1981)? Or, was public opinion driving the president and policy (Converse, 1987)? This study has defined the drug issue as a *symbolic crisis* in which "a combination of events and the responses of the government, the public and the media leads to a public definition of the issue as a problem of crisis proportions for a limited period of time" (Neuman, 1990, p. 169). The issue has also been classified as an *unobtrusive* issue in which the media should have a strong agenda-setting effect on public perceptions of importance (Zucker, 1978). However, the study has also classified the drug issue as a *concrete* issue, which also suggests that the media should have a strong agenda-setting effect on public salience (Yagade & Dozier, 1990). The permutations of effects are numerous and complex. The answer lies in the modeling and analysis of the interrelationships among these agendas over time.

UNIVARIATE ANALYSIS OF THE FIVE SERIES

The first step in the ARIMA analysis, which is discussed in detail in chapter 2 and Appendix B, is to model each of the series by itself. The first parameter to model is *trend* (d), which is the motion or trend in a specific direction, usually upward or downward, within a series, or, more specifically, any systematic change in the level of a time series (McCleary & Hay, 1980). The second component to model is the autoregressive parameter (p), which is the correlation in the error structure between observations. As shown in Table 6.1, the *autoregressive parameter p*, which is indicated by ϕ, is simply a correlation coefficient. The final parameter, the *moving average process*, is characterized by a finite persistence in the random shock. A random shock enters the system and then persists for no more than q observations before it vanishes entirely. In this analysis, a moving average parameter did not have to be modeled because of the nature of each of the series. The important thing to remember in the ARIMA modeling of the univariate series is that each of these parameters must be modeled, or mathematically determined and accounted for, before the relationships between the respective series can be examined. If these parameters are not adequately modeled, the findings concerning the relationships between the series will be inaccurate.

The ARIMA analysis of each of the univariate series offered interesting insights into the nature of the roller coaster ride through time for each of the measures (see Table 6.1). The ARIMA model for the public opinion series required first-order differencing to remove systematic trend and indicated a moderately strong first-order, autoregressive process—that is, a given month k was correlated or predicted by the preceding month ($k - 1$). The analysis also suggested a moderately strong first-order, autoregressive seasonal process at 2 months. The coefficients indicated a negative correlation for the seasonal component, suggesting that public opinion 2 months prior to a given month k, or $k - 2$, was inversely correlated to public opinion at month k.

The ARIMA model for the media-agenda series indicated a similar structure to the public-opinion series, but it included a very strong first-order, autoregressive process with a moderately strong first-order autoregressive seasonal process at 2 months. In addition, like public opinion, the coefficient of the seasonal component was negative, suggesting that media coverage 2 months prior to a given month k was inversely correlated to media coverage at month k.

TABLE 6.1
Univariate ARIMA Coefficients and Explained Variance

Time Series	ARIMA Term	Significant Coefficients	t-Ratio	R^2
1. Public opinion	$(1,1,0)(1,0,0)_2$	$\phi_1 = .33$	3.10	.892
		$\phi_2 = .33$	-3.11	
2. Media	$(1,0,0)(1,0,0)_2$	$\phi_1 = .76$	6.93	.442
		$\phi_2 = -.24$	-2.25	
3. President	$(1,0,0)$	$\phi_1 = .49$	5.11	.236
4. Policy	$(0,1,0)$			.971
5. Emergency room	$(0,1,0)(1,0,0)_3$	$\phi_3 = .48$	4.70	.983

The ARIMA model for the presidential agenda indicated a strong first-order autoregressive process, but the policy series had no significant autoregressive or moving-average parameters. The modeling of the policy series only required a first-order differencing to remove the systematic trend. The emergency-room series also required first-order differencing, but it also indicated a strong first-order, autoregressive seasonal process at 3 months. Unlike the public opinion and media time series, the seasonal component of the emergency-room series was positive, suggesting that the real-world cue measure 3 months prior to a given month k was positively correlated to the real-world cue measure at month k.

Table 6.1 also includes an estimate of the *explained variance* for each of the models, or the percentage of the variance that is explained by the ARIMA model of the series itself (see McCleary & Hay, 1980). This estimated explained variance was calculated by subtracting the variance of model residuals from the variance of the original variable and then dividing this difference by the variance of the original variable. The method is similar in logic and procedure to that proposed by McCleary and Hay to estimate explained variance of an ARIMA univariate model. The public-opinion ARIMA model explained almost 90% of the variance of the public opinion agenda, whereas the media and presidential agenda ARIMA models explained 44% and 24% of each series' variance, respectively. The extremely high explained variance for the policy series (97%) and emergency-room series (98%) are artifacts of the monthly estimating procedures used for the series (annual to monthly for the policy series, and quarterly to monthly for the emergency-room series) and offer support for the decision to only use these measures as independent variables in the bivariate and multivariate analyses.

GRANGER CAUSALITY: BIVARIATE ANALYSIS

After determining the ARIMA model for each series, the next step to the ultimate goal of developing a multivariate model of the relationship of agendas is to examine the *bivariate* (or respective pairs) of relationships of the drug-issue agendas. This bivariate analysis took each independently *prewhitened,* or modeled, series (Haugh & Box, 1977) and examined the cross-lagged correlations for each of the possible pairs of agendas (see Gonzenbach, 1992; Mark, 1979; Vandaele, 1983).

The concept of a cross-lagged correlation is actually very simple. As an example, let us examine the bivariate relationship between the public opinion series and the media series, where the public opinion series is treated as the independent series (the series that predicts the dependent series) and the media series is treated as the dependent series (the series that is predicted by the independent series). The cross-lagged correlation analysis simultaneously examines the relationship between the media series at a given month k and the public opinion series for each of the 12 months prior to the given month k, that is, k-1, k-2, k-3, and so on, and for the month k itself, which is called the *synchronous relationship* or the relationship at the same point in time. The relationship between the media at month k and public opinion at some previous month, such as k-2, is typically referred to as the relationship of public opinion at lag -2 on the media.

Based on the cross-lagged correlation analysis, the statistically significant lags of the respective independent series are then used as the independent variables to predict the respective dependent series in a simultaneous regression analysis using Yule–Walker estimation (SAS Institute, 1988). The simultaneous regression analysis also includes an analysis of the Durbin–Watson d-statistic as a double check for autocorrelation. The models did not indicate autocorrelation after the ARIMA modeling.

This simultaneous regression analysis is called a test of *Granger causality,* which is an F-test contrasting the incremental explained variance for each regression model (variance explained by predictors which are above that explained by the dependent series' univariate ARIMA model). Following are the possible outcomes for the Granger causality test:

1. A *one-way* causal relationship is determined when one time series explains the other, but the reverse does not occur.
2. A *feedback,* or reciprocal causal relationship occurs when two time series contribute equally to explain each other's variance when they are included in the regression equation of the other.
3. An *instantaneous causal link* occurs when the present and the past history of one time series contributes to increase the other variable's total variance explained.
4. The *absence* of Granger causality is assessed when neither of the two series increases the other's variance by including their past histories for the other. (Roger et al., 1991, pp. 26–27)

In these bivariate analyses and Granger causality tests, each of the possible combinations of the public opinion, media, and presidential series were examined. However, the policy and emergency-room series were only treated as independent variables because of the estimation problems noted previously. Therefore, the policy and emergency-room series were specified as control variables and each was used as an independent variable to predict the public opinion, media, and presidential series. The significant coefficients from this one-way analysis of the three dependent series were then used in the three multivariate analyses with the public opinion, media, and presidential series as the respective dependent series. Table 6.2 summarizes the results of the bivariate analysis and Granger causality tests for the specific hypotheses proposed in chapter 4.

The *first hypothesis* predicts that a two-way (feedback) effect will occur between the media and public opinion, but that the effect of the media on public opinion will occur more quickly (shorter time lag) than the effect of public opinion on the media. That is, the media and public opinion will affect each other, but the effect of the media on public opinion will take less time than the effect of public opinion on the

TABLE 6.2
Bivariate Analysis of Test and Control Variables

Dependent Series	Independent Series	Significant Coefficients (.05 level)	Standard Error	Total R_2	Incremental R_2
Test Variables					
1. Media agenda	Public opinion	4.87_{t-0}	1.11	.686	.244
		4.20_{t-1}	1.11		
		3.18_{t-4}	1.11		
Public opinion	Media agenda	0.04_{t-0}	0.01	.924	.032
		-0.02_{t-8}	0.01		
2. Public opinion	President agenda	-0.29_{t-6}	0.11	.913	.021
		0.24_{t-8}	0.11		
President agenda	Public opinion	None		.236	.000
3. Media agenda	President agenda	4.96_{t-0}	1.28	.582	.139
President agenda	Media agenda	0.04_{t-0}	0.01	.618	.382
		0.02_{t-1}	0.01		
		0.02_{t-3}	0.01		
Control Variables					
4. Public opinion	Policy agenda	-0.13_{t-9}	0.05	.910	.018
Media agenda	Policy agenda	None			
President agenda	Policy agenda	None			
5. Public opinion	Emergency room	0.01_{t-10}	0.01	.908	.016
Media agenda	Emergency room	None			
President agenda	Emergency room	None			

media. This hypothesis was not clearly supported. A two-way (or feedback) relationship was not found between public opinion and the media. The Granger causality test suggested an *instantaneous causal link*; public opinion at any given month k (lag 0) and public opinion one month and four months prior to month k (lags -1 and -4) explained media coverage at month k, but not the reverse. In addition, the present and past history of the public opinion series increased the explained variance of the prewhitened media series by 24%.

The *second hypothesis* predicts that a two-way (feedback) effect will occur between the president and public opinion, but the effect of the president on public opinion will occur more quickly (shorter time lag) than the effect of public opinion on the president. That is, presidential public relations activity and public opinion will affect each other, but the effect of the president on public opinion will take less time than the effect of public opinion on presidential activity. This hypothesis was not supported. The Granger causality test suggested the *absence* of Granger causality; neither of the two series increased the other's explained variance by including their past histories for the other. Public opinion did not predict presidential public-relations activity, nor did presidential public-relations activity predict public opinion.

The *third hypothesis* predicts that the media will have a one-way effect on the president; that is, media coverage explains presidential public-relations activity, but presidential activity does not explain media coverage. This hypothesis was partially supported. The media's agenda predicted the president's public-relations agenda; however, the effect was an *instantaneous causal link*. The present (lag 0) and past history (lags -1 and -3) of media coverage predicted the president's public relations activities. Plus, the present and past history of the media series increased the explained variance of the prewhitened presidential series by 38%.

The *fourth hypothesis* predicts that the policy agenda will have a one-way effect on the media agenda; that is, policy explains media coverage, but media coverage does not explain policy. This hypothesis was partially supported. The policy agenda 9 months prior to a given month k mildly predicted public opinion at month k, although the explained variance of the prewhitened public-opinion series increased by only about 2%. Interestingly, the significant coefficient at lag -9 is negative, indicating an inverse relationship between policy and public opinion. Finally, the policy agenda predicted neither the media agenda nor the presidential public-relations agenda.

The *fifth hypothesis* predicts the real-world cue agenda will have a one-way effect on the president, the media, and public opinion agenda; that is, reality explains presidential public relations activities, media coverage, and public opinion, but the president, the media, and public opinion do not explain the real-world cue. This hypothesis was also partially supported. The real-world cue measure 10 months prior to a given month k predicted public opinion at month k and minimally increased the explained variance of the prewhitened public opinion series by about 2%; however, the emergency-room measure predicted neither the media agenda nor the presidential agenda.

The bivariate analysis and Granger causality tests indicated three significant relationships: (a) the real-world cues at lag -10 positively predicted public opinion, and policy at lag -9 inversely predicted public opinion; (b) public opinion at lag 0, lag -1, and lag -4 positively predicted the media agenda; and (c) the media agenda at lag 0, lag -1, and lag -3 positively predicted the president's public-relations agenda. Based on these findings, the public-opinion, media, and presidential agendas were each examined as the dependent series in a multivariate analysis.

MULTIVARIATE ANALYSIS AND MODELS

Based on the findings of the bivariate analysis and Granger causality tests, three multivariate analyses were conducted. The first analysis used the policy agenda at lag -9 and the real-world cue agenda at lag -10 to predict public opinion. The second analysis used public opinion at lags 0, -1, and -4 to predict the media agenda; the policy agenda at lag -9 and the real-world cue at lag -10 were also included as control variables. The third analysis used the media agenda at lags 0, -1, and -3 to predict the presidential public relations agenda, and also included the policy agenda at lag -9 and the real-world cue at lag -10 as control variables.

Public Opinion

The public opinion series was inversely predicted by the policy agenda at lag -9 and positively predicted by the emergency-room measure at lag -10, much like the bivariate analyses. Compared to the bivariate analyses, the explained and incremental variance were virtually the same at 90% and 16% respectively (see Table 6.3 and Fig. 6.1).

The findings suggest three important considerations. First, in this study, public opinion is predicted by its own past history (see Fig. 6.1). Public opinion in any given month k is predicted strongly and positively by public opinion in the prior month (k-1) is also strongly and inversely predicted by public opinion in the month

TABLE 6.3
Analysis of Public Opinion, Media Agenda, and Presidential Public-Relations
Agenda as Dependent Series

Dependent Series	Independent Series	Significant Coefficients (.05 Level)	Standard Error	Total R^2	Incremental R^2
1. Public opinion	Public agenda	-0.13_{t-9}	0.05	.908	.016
	Emergency room	0.01_{t-10}	0.01		
2. Media agenda	Public opinion	5.04_{t-0}	1.10	.680	.238
		4.40_{t-1}	1.10		
		2.83_{t-4}	1.10		
3. President agenda	Media agenda	0.03_{t-0}	0.01	.598	.362
		0.02_{t-1}	0.01		
		0.02_{t-3}	0.01		

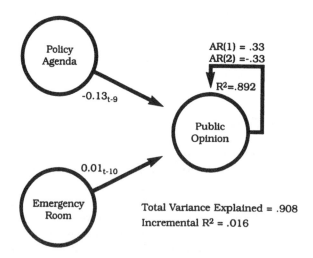

FIG. 6.1.   Analysis of public opinion as dependent series ($N = 84$ months).

prior to that (k-2). Second, public opinion in any given month k is mildly and inversely predicted by federal expenditures 9 months prior to the month k. This seems to make intuitive sense. If the federal government is increasing expenditures on the issue, the public becomes less concerned 9 months later; if the federal government is spending less on the issue, the public becomes more concerned 9 months later. Third, public opinion in any given month k is mildly and positively predicted by the severity of the real-world cue measure of emergency-room admissions 10 months prior to the month k. Again, this seems to make intuitive sense. As the severity of the real-world measure increases, so does public concern 10 months later; as the severity of reality measure decreases, so does public concern 10 months later.

The most interesting finding concerning public opinion is that it is not driven by the media nor by presidential public relations activity. Many studies document this agenda-setting effect of the mass media salience affecting public salience, although there are limitations and qualifications (Leff, Protess, & Brooks, 1986; O'Keefe, 1985; T. Smith, 1980; K. A. Smith, 1987; Steadman & Cocozza, 1977). One study suggested that increased media attention to drugs produced a similar result for public opinion of drugs (Beniger, 1978). A study relating media content and public opinion about drugs from 1972–1986 indicated that the more the media emphasized drugs the more people listed drugs as the most important problem facing the country; the agenda-setting effects were then most pronounced during the weeks immediately preceding the poll and about 3 months before the poll (Shoemaker, Wanta, & Leggett, 1989). However, agenda-setting research also indicates that issues can rise without media attention (Sohn, 1978), and that they can remain important after press attention has faded (Weaver, Graber, McCombs, & Eyal, 1981).

Beniger (1978) also found evidence that press attention to illicit drugs was related to a decline in drug use under some conditions. Experimental evidence indicates that the agenda-setting effect is unidirectional (Behr & Iyengar, 1985), whereas Kepplinger et al. (1989) found that press coverage preceded public opinion. However, coverage also followed public opinion, although it took an opposite stance. Rogers and Dearing (1988) suggested that there is "undoubtedly a two-way, mutually dependent relationship between the public agenda and the media agenda" (p. 571). This is supported in a study by Erbring, Goldenberg, and Miller (1980) which indicates that the influence of the public agenda on the press agenda is a gradual, long-term process through which generalized news values are developed. Conversely, the influence of the media agenda on the public agenda for a specific news item would appear to be a more direct, immediate cause–effect relationship, particularly when the public has few alternatives, such as direct experience.

This caveat about direct experience may be the key point to consider regarding the drug issue. This study's categorization of the drug issue as an unobtrusive issue in which events create issues with which people ordinarily have no direct experience (Zucker, 1978) may be incorrect. The analyses, which have controlled for important competing explanations and the mathematical properties of the respective series, point only to federal policy and reality as predictors of public opinion. It is possible that Zucker was incorrect; drugs may have landed on the doorsteps of America and this real-world experience and resulting policy action became the important, although mild, predictors of public opinion. The results of the few studies that have examined the role of real-world cues suggest this may be the case. MacKuen (1981) found that real-world cue measures confounded the media-agenda-moving-toward-public-agenda relationships and that there was a direct influence of real-world cues on the public agenda, without this relationship going through the media agenda. Similarly, Erbring et al. (1980) found that real-world indictors were significantly related to public salience of the issues.

Media Agenda

The introduction of the policy and real-world cue measure into the model predicting that the media agenda had minimal effect. As in the bivariate analysis, the media agenda was still predicted by public opinion at lags 0, -1, and -4 and the explained and incremental variance remained virtually the same at 68% and 24%, respectively (see Table 6.3 and Fig. 6.2).

The findings suggest two important considerations. First, in this study the media agenda is predicted by its own past history (see Fig. 6.1). Media coverage in any given month k is predicted strongly and positively by media coverage in the prior month (k-1) and is also strongly and inversely predicted by media coverage in the month prior to that (k-2). Second, media coverage in any given month k is strongly and positively predicted by public opinion in that same month k, as well as in the month immediately preceding (k-1) and in the month 4 months prior (k-4) to it.

Research suggests that there is "undoubtedly a two-way, mutually dependent relationship between the public agenda and the media agenda" (Rogers & Dearing, 1987, p. 571) and that the effect of the media on the public agenda is generally

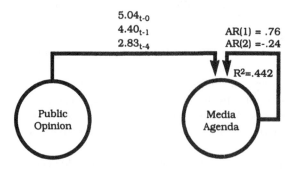

FIG. 6.2. Analysis of the media agenda as the dependent series (N = 84 months).

direct and immediate, whereas the effect of public opinion on the media is a gradual and long-term process (Erbring et al. 1980). In this analysis, it is impossible to completely unravel the causal order of the relationship between the media and public opinion in the synchronous month k because the unit of analysis in the study is a monthly measure. For example, it is impossible to determine if a news report in the first week of the month was affecting public opinion in the third week of the month, or if public opinion, measured in the second week of the month, was affecting media coverage in the fourth week of the month. We suspect that Rogers and Dearing are correct; there is probably a two-way, mutual relationship occurring within that month k; that is, each agenda is affecting the other. Although this is speculative, the evidence in this study tends to support the conclusion that public opinion has more of an effect on the media than the reverse, and that the effect of public opinion on the media is also gradual and long-term—in this case 1 and 4 months.

Presidential Agenda

The introduction of the policy and real-world cue measure into the model that predicted the presidential agenda had minimal effect. As in the bivariate analysis, the presidential agenda was still predicted by the media agenda at lags 0, -1, and -3. The explained variance decreased slightly from 62% to 60% and incremental variance decreased slightly from 38% to 36% (see Table 6.3 and Fig. 6.3).

The findings suggest two important considerations. First, in this study the presidential agenda is predicted by its own past history (see Fig. 6.1). Presidential public-relations activity in any given month k is predicted strongly and positively by presidential activity in the prior month (k-1). Second, presidential PR activity in any given month k is strongly and positively predicted by media coverage in that same month k, as well as in the month immediately preceding (k-1) and in the month 3 months prior (k-3).

As with the relationship between the media and public opinion, it is impossible to completely sort out the order of effects between the media and the president in the synchronous month k; we again speculate that there is probably a two-way effect

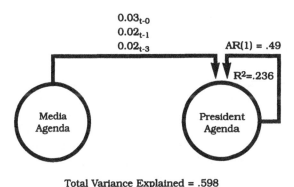

0.03_{t-0}
0.02_{t-1}
0.02_{t-3} $AR(1) = .49$

$R^2 = .236$

Media Agenda   President Agenda

Total Variance Explained = .598
Incremental R^2 = .362

FIG. 6.3. Analysis of the presidential agenda as the dependent series ($N = 84$ months).

TABLE 6.4
Analysis of the Agendas in the Reagan and Bush Presidencies

Dependent Series	Independent Series	Significant Coefficients (.05 Level)	Standard Error	Total R^2	Incremental R^2
Reagan Administration (July 1984–December 1988)					
1. Public opinion	Policy agenda	None		.892	.000
	Emergency room	None			
2. Media agenda	Public opinion	6.13_{t-1}	2.29	.656	.213
3. President agenda	Media agenda	0.04_{t-1}	0.01	.560	.325
Bush Administration (January 1989–June 1991)					
1. Public opinion	Policy agenda	-0.19_{t-9}	0.08	.943	.051
	Emergency room	0.02_{t-10}	0.01		
2. Media agenda	Public opinion	5.19_{t-0}	1.23	.859	.417
		4.52_{t-1}	1.23		
		4.61_{t-4}	1.23		
3. President agenda	Media agenda	0.05_{t-0}	0.01	.672	.437

occurring within any given month. However, the findings of the study tend to support the notion that the president is following media coverage 3 months prior, 1 month prior, and within the given month k; that is, when the media speaks, the president listens—not the reverse.

A COMPARISON OF THE REAGAN AND BUSH PRESIDENCIES

The final element of the analysis examined if the relationships of the agendas varied with the presidencies of Reagan and Bush. The analysis utilized the same analysis as that of the multivariate analysis; however, the time frames of the two administrations were used as a control variable in the analysis. In the time frame of the study, the Reagan administration comprised the period from July 1984 to December 1988, and the Bush administration comprised the period from January 1988 to June 1991.

The analysis indicated some important differences in the relationship of the agendas during the two administrations (Table 6.4). In the Reagan years, the policy agenda and real-world cue agenda did not predict public opinion, whereas in the Bush administration the relationship was very similar to the findings of the multivariate analysis for the entire period of the study. In the Bush years, policy was again inversely related to public opinion at lag -9 and the real-world cue was positively related to public opinion at lag -10. In addition, the explained and incremental variance increased slightly for the Bush years as compared to the entire time period of the study. This tends to support the conclusion that the policy agenda and the real-world cues played a more significant role in the Bush years than in either the Reagan years or the entire time frame of the study. Given the steady increase of both of these measures in the latter parts of the study's time cycle, the finding seems logical.

A similar relationship was indicated for the public-opinion-media model. In the Reagan years, only public opinion at lag -1 predicted the media agenda, and the explained and incremental variance again decreased in relation to the analysis of the entire period of the study. In the Bush years, public opinion at lags 0, -1, and -4 predicted media coverage, and, compared to the analysis for the entire period of the study, the explained variance of the model in the Bush years increased by 18%, as did the incremental variance. This supports the conclusion that public opinion played a more significant role in the media's agenda in the Bush years than in either the Reagan years or in the entire time frame of the study. Given the rapid rise in public concern about drugs during the Bush administration, this finding also seems logical.

Finally, the effect of the media agenda predicting the presidential public relations agenda during each administration offers some important information. In the Reagan years, the president was only affected by the media at lag -1, compared to lags 0, -1, and -3 for the entire period of the study and to lag 0 for the Bush years. As with the other models, the explained and incremental variance of the model in the Reagan years is less than that of the entire time frame of the study. President Reagan followed the media, but it took him a month to do so. In addition, compared to the analysis of the entire period of the study, the explained variance of the model in the Bush years increased by 10% and the incremental variance for the model increased by 8%. This difference suggests that the media played a more important role on the presidential agenda in the Bush years than in either the Reagan years or in the entire time frame of the study. Based on this data and the content analysis findings, it is concluded that President Bush reacted more immediately to the media agenda and possibly had a more immediate two-way relationship with the media with a given month, but that in general the presidents followed rather than led the media.

The findings of this analysis of the relationships controlling for the presidential administration indicated that all the significant relationships were more heightened in the Bush administration than in the Reagan administration or in the entire time frame of the study. Based on the relationships among the key variables, the findings suggest that increasing real-world problems in the later phase of the study were more important to the public, that this heightened public concern caught the media's attention more in the later phase of the time frame, that the increased media attention in the Bush years affected the president more, and that President Bush reacted more quickly to the media's cues and in turn responded to these cues more immediately than did President Reagan.

CONCLUSION

This chapter has addressed the study's third and fourth research questions. After modeling each univariate series and conducting Granger Causality tests on the bivariate series, three multivariate models were examined: the first used the public opinion series as the dependent measure, the second used the media series as the dependent measure, and the third used the presidential series as the dependent measure.

The multivariate analyses suggest the following about the relationships among the drug issue agendas. Public opinion is minimally and inversely predicted by the policy agenda at lag -9 and minimally predicted by the real-world cue at lag -10. These significant predictors only increased the model's explained variance by about 2% compared to the variance that is accounted for by the univariate public opinion series itself. In general, the government's policy actions 9 months prior inversely and mildly predict public concern and the reality of the issue 10 months prior minimally and positively predicts the public's concern about drugs as the country's most important problem.

The media agenda is predicted by public opinion at lag -4, lag -1, and lag 0. These significant predictors increased the model's explained variance by almost 24% compared to the variance that is accounted for by the univariate media series itself. In general, the public's concern about the issue 4 months prior, 1 month prior, and during the same month predict the media's agenda concerning drugs. In addition, the presidential public relations agenda is predicted by the media agenda at lag -3, lag -1, and lag 0. These significant predictors increased the model's explained variance by about 36% compared to the variance that is accounted for by the univariate presidential series. In general, the media's focus on drugs 3 months prior, 1 month prior, and during the same month predict the presidential public-relations agenda.

The cumulative picture of these three multivariate analyses tends to suggest that the reality of the issue, and the government's actions to address this reality with dollars, slowly and mildly affect public concern about the issue. This public concern more immediately and strongly affects the media's focus on the issue, which, in turn, affects presidential public relations efforts about the issue.

How these relationships among the agendas differed during the Reagan and Bush presidencies suggested some important findings. First, the policy agenda and the real-world cue agenda did not predict public opinion in the Reagan presidency, but they did mildly predict public opinion in the Bush presidency, suggesting that increased policy action and the severity of the drug issue played a more significant role in the Bush years. Second, public opinion had a more pronounced affect on the media's agenda in the Bush years, suggesting the effect of the dramatic increase in public concern on the media during Bush's presidency. Finally, the increased media attention in the Bush years affected President Bush more than the media affected President Reagan, and President Bush reacted more quickly to the media's cues and in turn responded to these cues more immediately than did President Reagan.

Chapter 7

The Drug Issue, 1984–1991: Conclusions and Implications

The objective of this study was to examine the drug issue from mid-1984 to mid-1991, using a more extensive theory of agenda setting in order to see how drug-related issues and events and the corresponding agendas affect the handling of issues. This chapter places these findings within the context of the agenda-setting research and seeks to make a little sense of this sometimes necessarily detailed and statistically driven analysis.

AGENDA-SETTING RESEARCH

In 1922, American journalist and social commentator Walter Lippmann (1922) suggested that the press is a spotlight that constantly scans the environment for news. As events occur, the spotlight shifts its focus. Lippmann argued that the media's spotlight selectively frames and creates our mental pictures of the world, a world that is often outside our direct experience. Although his conceptualization of media effects offers a rich foundation for theoretical research, the first generation of scientific mass-communication research ended in 1960 with the publication of Klapper's (1960) *The Effects of Mass Communication,* which basically concluded that there are no direct effects of the media on individuals, particularly on attitudes and opinions (McCombs, 1993).

Against this research tradition, McCombs and Shaw (1972) returned to Lippmann's conceptualization of media effects and tested the specific proposition that through their selection and display of the news, the mass media influence public perception and salience of what are the important issues of the day. More specifically, they argued the causal assertion that over time the priorities of the media become the priorities of the public. This basic premise has spawned more than 200 empirical studies over the last 25 years.

Based on this research tradition, in 1988 Rogers and Dearing modeled a broad conceptualization of the agenda process that incorporates three main components: media agenda setting, in which the main dependent variable is the media's news agenda; public agenda setting, in which the main dependent variable is the content and order of topics in the public agenda; and policy agenda setting, the distinctive aspect of which is its concern with policy as a response to both the media agenda and the public agenda. The model also comprises three other components: influence agents, such as gatekeepers, influential media, and spectacular news events; personal experience and interpersonal communication about the issue of concern; and real-world cues about the importance of an issue, which offer an objective measure of the severity of the issue devoid of the fictions, or the representations of the issue created by people. This study utilized this model to address the complex sets of relationships concerning the drug issue from 1984 to 1991 in the United States.

Agenda setting is by definition a time-related process, yet it has often been approached as a nonprocess because it has been generally treated as one part of the general quest by mass-communication scholars for media effects. A new component of agenda-setting research turned to ARIMA modeling to address agenda setting as a process and to control for the important mathematical properties of stationarity and autocorrelation in time-series analysis. Again, this study of the drug issue is but a part of this new component of agenda-setting research.

Primarily, this study of the drug issue used Rogers and Dearing's (1988) broadened agenda-setting model to examine Lippmann's (1922) concepts of how the media and other influence agents, such as the president, selectively frame perceptions of the reality of the issue. It then incorporated time-series analysis with ARIMA modeling to address key methodological concerns about stationarity and autocorrelation and to unravel the causal order of relationships among the issue's primary agendas while controlling for the effects of other important measures.

THE STRUCTURING AND RELATIONSHIP OF AGENDAS

Media coverage of the drug issue was like a steadily rising roller coaster ride, structured by drug issues and events, both real and politically contrived, that plummeted in the early part of 1991. Presidential public-relations efforts were also a roller coaster ride through time, yet took a few more severe dips and turns. Like the media, however, the presidential ride also came to a crawl in the early part of 1991.

In the preproblem stage (July 1984–May 1986), the media initially structured coverage around the rather unobtrusive, yet concrete, events of the drug-related problems of prominent sports figures, the John deLorean case, and the death of Salazar. These real events captured the media's attention, although they did not create the public opinion that drugs were the country's most important problem.

However, the political issues surrounding drug testing and NIDA's public infor-mation campaign about cocaine, combined with the increasing problems of drugs in professional sports during the latter part of this stage, captured the attention of both the media and the public. Although President Reagan spoke out about drugs less than three times a month in the preproblem stage, in the early part of the stage his interest was rising, in sync with his wife's concerns about education and prevention. These topics did not capture the attention of the public. However, the "reality" roller coaster concerning the severity of the problem was just pulling out of the gate at the end of this stage.

In the discovery stage (June 1986–December 1987), media coverage of political issues and the very real and concrete examples of cocaine's effects, exemplified by the death of Len Bias, drove the content of coverage. Media coverage and public opinion rose sharply after the Bias death and President Reagan's war on drugs, which focused on the political but again very concrete issues of testing, military use, and highly visible internal and external administrative actions. After the summer of 1986, presidential attention, media coverage, and public concern de-creased; however, the reality of drugs, as measured by the number of cocaine-related emergency-room admissions, steadily and quickly mounted to a peak of horrors.

By the beginning of the plateau stage (January 1988–January 1990), the issue took on new life for the media, the president, and the public. Media coverage in this stage was structured around the very real-world issue of drug-related violence and crime and the very politically driven events of Colombia, Noriega, and Bush's plan, war, and drug czar. During the first half of 1988, presidential attention arose as Reagan focused on Nicaragua and Manuel Noriega, AIDS, the Omnibus Drug Initiative of 1988, and funding issues concerning enforcement and education.

Presidential attention then quieted until President Bush's inauguration in Janu-ary 1989, when his drug-related efforts rose dramatically under the guidance of William Bennett. Bush announced his war plan that focused on education, treat-ment, interdiction, and enforcement, and he began to focus on the issues of violence and crime and the mounting problems in Colombia. After public concern rose in the summer of 1989, President Bush addressed the nation in September about his National Drug Control Strategy. His activities seemed to have a strong affect on the media's coverage of the issue and and his efforts seemed to heighten public concern.

After September 1989, Bush's public-relations efforts and public interest de-clined sharply; media interest declined until January 1990, when it engaged in a flurry of activity concerning Bush's administrative actions and emerging claims of success in his war on drugs. During this stage, the reality of the problem dramati-cally increased, but then declined in the latter part of 1989. This seemed to tie in to the decline in interest of the media, the president and the public; however, the decline was short-lived as the reality of the issue remounted early 1991—the latter part of the decline stage.

In the decline stage (February 1990–June 1991), the attention of the media, the public, and the president all quickly dropped. The media's coverage in this stage continued to focus on the obtrusive and concrete issue of drug-related violence and crime and the political events surrounding Mayor Barry, the drug lords of Colombia, the indictment of Manuel Noriega, and the transition of power in the drug czar's office. The tone of the content in this stage moved from the problems of the issue to the success of the political efforts to control the problem. Amidst proclamations of success, President Bush began to focus on community action and voluntarism in his Points of Light program, much like President Reagan's focus at the beginning of the emergence of the problem. However, the continued coverage of violence and crime and the frequency of emergency-room admissions for cocaine-related injury continued to signal the problem of drugs in the communities of the United States.

INFLUENCES OF AGENDAS OVER TIME

The causal order of the relationships of the primary agendas of the drug issue, as presented in Rogers and Dearing's (1987) broadened agenda-setting model (see Fig. 1.1), is unraveled in this analysis through the use of Granger causality tests and ARIMA modeling. This statistical approach controls for the important properties of stationarity and autocorrelation within each agenda and it addresses the causal order of the key relationships while controlling for the important competing variables.

This macrolevel analysis paints a very interesting and important portrait of how these agendas influence each other over time, as summarized in Fig. 7.1. In general, the findings suggest that the public's attention to the issue is first driven by the severity of the problem and the government's response to the severity of the problem, although the relationships are very mild. The awareness process begins

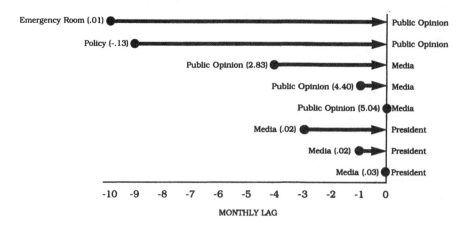

FIG. 7.1. Summary of multivariate analyses: Influences of agendas over time.

with the real-world cue measure of the severity of the issue, which mildly influences public opinion 10 months prior to any given month k. As an example, the public's view of the drug issue as being the most important issue facing the country in December 1987 was mildly and positively predicted by the severity of the issue in February 1987.

Conversely, public opinion in any given month k, or in this case December 1987, was mildly and negatively predicted by policy actions 9 months prior to this time, in this case March 1987. The negative relationship suggests that if the intensity of policy action was increasing, the public was becoming less concerned or vice versa. Although the relationships are very mild, the findings tend to suggest that the study's initial categorization of the drug issue was incorrect. The drug issue was not an unobtrusive issue for the public; rather, the obtrusive nature of the problem throughout the communities of the United States and the government's response to this problem both heralded the public's awareness of the issue as the most important problem facing the country.

Next, the public's awareness of the problem influenced the attention of the media to the problem, again suggesting the obtrusive nature of the problem and pointing to the important role the media can play as a conduit in grassroots democracy. The findings suggest that public opinion 4 months and 1 month prior to any given month k influenced the media's agenda for that month k. Using the previous example, media attention in December 1987 was positively influenced by public opinion both in August 1987 and November 1987. In addition, media attention in a given month k was also correlated with public opinion for that month k; using the example, media attention in December 1987 was correlated with public opinion in December 1987. As noted previously, it is impossible to determine which agenda is the predictor agenda for this relationship within a given month (synchronous relationship) given the aggregate, monthly nature of the data. In general, the findings offer support that public opinion influenced media attention 4 months and 1 month prior to that time and that the two agendas influenced each other for any synchronous month.

In many ways this influence of public opinion on the media was personified by the conversation between political activist Jesse Jackson and A. M. Rosenthal, executive director of *The New York Times,* in the fall of 1985. Jackson, acting as a spokesperson for the public, met with Rosenthal to discuss the devastating, destructive forces of drugs, especially cocaine and crack cocaine. Due to Jackson's spotlighting of the problem, *The Times* finally addressed the drug issue as an important social problem and began to regularly focus on the problem in its coverage. Like Jackson, the public's awareness of the issue as an important problem turned the media's spotlight on it from 1984 to 1991. This influence of public opinion on the media agenda points to the power of the public in the garnering of attention for an obtrusive issue and suggests that the media can be—when persuaded regarding the importance of an issue—an important conduit in carrying the public's message of concern.

The final important finding of the analysis suggests that the media did indeed carry the public's message of concern—to the president! The findings suggest that the media agenda 3 months and 1 month prior to any given month k influenced the presidential public relations agenda for that month k. Using the previous example, presidential attention in December 1987 was positively influenced by media attention both in September 1987 and November 1987. In addition, presidential attention in a given month k was also correlated with media attention for that month k; using the example, presidential attention in December 1987 was correlated with media attention in December 1987. As noted previously, it is impossible to determine which agenda is the predictor agenda for this relationship within a given month (synchronous relationship) given the aggregate, monthly nature of the data. However, the findings offer support that the media agenda influenced presidential public relations 3 months and 1 month prior to that time and that the two agendas influenced each other for any synchronous month.

This finding paints a picture of the president as a follower rather than a leader concerning the obtrusive drug issue and the analysis of the analysis of the differences between the Reagan and Bush administrations pointed to some key differences between the two presidents. First, the policy agenda and the real-world cue agenda did not predict public opinion in the Reagan presidency, but did mildly predict public opinion in the Bush presidency, suggesting that increased policy action and the severity of the drug issue played a more significant role in the Bush years. Second, public opinion had a more pronounced affect on the media's agenda in the Bush years, suggesting the effect of the dramatic increase in public concern on the media during Bush's presidency. Third, the increased media attention in the Bush years affected President Bush more than the media had affected President Reagan. In addition, Bush reacted more quickly to the media's cues and in turn responded to these cues more immediately than did Reagan.

This presidential responsiveness of the president to the media's agenda is supported by other studies that have examined the relationship between the presidential issue agenda as presented in State of the Union speeches and the media's agenda of issues before, during and after these speeches (Gilberg, Eyal, McCombs, & Nichols, 1980; Wanta, Stephenson, Turk, & McCombs, 1989). Although the results are sometimes conflicting, the findings suggest that the president's agenda of issues in the State of the Union speeches often followed the media's agenda of issues. For the drug issue, the evidence is clear: The president responded to the media spotlight.

At a very macrolevel perspective, the drug issue seems to be an obtrusive issue in which the reality of the problem and governmental policy responses to the issue mildly influenced public concern. This public concern, in turn, captured the media's attention, which then captured the attention of the president, who was much more of a follower than a leader concerning the drug issue from 1984 to 1991.

THEORETICAL CONSIDERATIONS AND IMPLICATIONS

After all is said and done, the real-world problem of the drug issue seemed to be the ultimate defining agent for public, media, and presidential attention from 1984 to 1991. The media agenda, the presidential public relations agenda, and measures of public opinion as drugs being the most important problem facing the country are all measures of perceptions about the importance of the issue. Underlying them all were the horrors of how drugs had affected communities and the American people's families and lives. This underlying relationship was confirmed by the analysis of the interactions of agendas, which indicate that the real-world problems of drugs entered the public consciousness and gradually defined people's perceptions of the problem months later, as did expenditures of the government, which inversely affected public perceptions months after the fact. This public concern then crept into the media's agenda and defined the media's salience of the issue as a topic worthy of coverage. In turn, the media's salience of the issue entered the presidential consciousness and defined presidential efforts to tackle the problem as an important administration issue.

The issue failed to resonate for the public, the media, and the president at the beginning and end of the study's time frame when the reality of the issue did not seem severe; as the real-world severity of the issue mounted, however, it drove the attention of the public, then the media, and then the president in a dance of mutually reinforcing effects that ultimately drove the issue to crisis proportions for each. The dance was ultimately centered around one issue—the appalling details of a major social problem that destroyed lives and families. Although all were not affected, few did not have a close experience with the issue. However, whereas the drug problem was about a single issue, the dance took on many forms and twists. The media tended to prefer its vivid images and numerous personalities, all of which seemed conducive to front-page news and 20-second sound bites. In the beginning, the media focused on rather surreal aspects of the issue, but soon turned to more reality-based reporting. The symbolic war against drugs ultimately became a real war—both at home and abroad—of violence and crime. These topics garnered the attention of the media and a new president who also had a war plan. When the reality measures offered a glimpse of hope that the issue was waning, media interest declined and presidential public relations returned to the rhetoric of voluntarism and community action. The public also turned their attention elsewhere; however, when the severity of the issue again mounted at the end of the cycle, only the public raised its head, although slightly and briefly, in concern.

If the drug issue was driven by the severity of the issue from 1984 to 1991, then one must ask why the issue is not at the forefront of media, presidential, and public attention today. Drugs are still a major national problem and drug-use figures suggest an increase in usage. The answer to this is that in a world with numerous social issues and problems, reality may not be enough to hold the spotlight of attention for the public, the media, or the president. The study's initial categorization of the drug issue was incorrect; the drug issue was not an unobtrusive issue for the public from 1984 to 1991—it ultimately entered our communities and homes as well as our newspapers and television sets. However, as suggested by Neuman (1990), the drug issue was also a symbolic crisis in which a combination of events and the responses of the government, the public, and the media led to a public definition of the issue as a problem of crisis proportions for a limited period of time. In essence, the drug issue was driven by a gestalt of events and attention that faded, although the severity of the issue did not. The public agenda is a zero-sum game in which issues move in and out of focus; the drug issue moved onto the agenda in a swirling dance of attention driven by the real-world severity of the issue. Then new issues, such as the Persian Gulf, the economy, and crime, became the new dance partners (Shaw & McCombs, 1989; Zhu, 1992).

The drug issue from 1984 to 1991 seemed to have a product life cycle in which the issue emerged, peaked, and then faded from the store shelf. The importance of the issue drove public attention, which influenced the media and then the president to respond and to repackaged the product as its numerous events and issues unfolded. However, the public faces numerous problems, and the media constantly look for new news, some of which leads to public salience and some of which responds to public salience. In addition, presidents want to be capable leaders and to secure reelection. By 1991, the public turned their attention to other pressing problems, the media turned their spotlight elsewhere, and the president seemed content to claim victory and move onto other problems that would provide a much simpler solution than this almost no-win issue. Without some major, change in the drug issue, it seems doomed to a smaller, dustier corner of the great grocery store shelf of issues.

Given the findings of this study, the conclusion made about the drug issue in 1992 is still supported:

> While the process appears complex and intertwined...the drug issue was a cyclical process driven by the reality of events and the reflected images of information campaigns and press and political concerns. The trend in opinion, when viewed in relation to these events and images, suggests that the public opinion process, as measured through the lens of public opinion polls, is a matter of public perceptions of the reality of the issue and of the pseudo-realities of information campaigns and presidential and press attention, which have their origins back in the heart of public concern. (Gonzenbach, 1992, pp. 143–144)

Appendix A: Summary of Public Opinion Surveys

Summary of Public Opinion Surveys

Date	ID	Co.	Pop	Size	Meth	MP	Form	% Sample	% Survey	% Adjust	% Used
JUN84	USGALLUP.1235.Q02A	GALLUP	NA	1522	PH	23	OPEN	104	2	2	2.0
JUL84	ESTIMATED										1.4
AUG84	USGALLUP.083084.R1	GALLUP	NA	1585	PH	11	OPEN	114	1	0.9	0.9
SEP84	USGALLUP.124.Q03A	GALLUP	NA	1521	PH	8	OPEN	105	1	1	1.0
	USGALLUP.1242.Q03A	GALLUP	NA	1518	PH	22	OPEN	100	1		
OCT84	USGALLUP.1242A.Q08D	GALLUP	NA	1590	PH	1	OPEN	120	2	1.6	1.6
NOV84	ESTIMATED										1.7
DEC84	ESTIMATED										1.7
JAN85	USGALLUP.235.-1.R2A	GALLUP	NA	1528	PH	26	OPEN	115	2	1.7	1.7
FEB85	ESTIMATED										2.4
MAR85	CRISTQ85	CAM REP	NA	1405	PR	15	OPEN	100	3	3.0	3.0
APR85	ESTIMATED										4
MAY85	USGALLUP.062385.R1	GALLUP	NA	1528	PH	18	OPEN	119	6	5.0	5.0
JUN85	CR2NDQ85	CAM REP	NA	1405	PR	15	OPEN	100	2	2.0	2.0
JUL85	ESTIMATED										2.0
AUG85	ESTIMATED										2.0
SEP85	CR3RDQ85	CAM REP	NA	1405	PR	15	OPEN	100	2	2.0	2.0
OCT85	USGALLUP.1110885.R1	GALLUP	NA	1540	PH	12	OPEN	114	3	2.6	2.6
NOV85	ESTIMATED										2.3
DEC85	CR4THQ85	CAM REP	NA	1405	PR	15	OPEN	100	2	2.0	2.0
JAN86	USABC.214.R04	ABC	NA	504	PH	25	OPEN	100	0	0.0	0.0
FEB86	ESTIMATED										1.5
MAR86	ESTIMATED										1.5
APR86	USCBSNYT.041486.R04	CBS/NYT	NA	1601	PH	8	OPEN	100	3	3.0	3.0
MAY86	ESTIMATED										4.1
JUN86	USNBCWSJ.373086.R1	NBC/WSJ	NA	1599	PH	2	CLOSED	100	12	5.2	5.2
JUL86	ESTIMATED										9.1
AUG86	USCBSNYT.080086.R02	CBS/NYT	NA	1210	PH	19	OPEN	100	13	13.0	13.0

Summary of Public Opinion Surveys (continued)

Date	ID	Co.	Pop	Size	Meth	MP	Form	% Sample	% Survey	% Adjust	% Used
SEP86	USNBCWSJ.121986.R23	NBC/WSJ	NA	2139	PH	21	CLOSED	100	20	8.6	8.8
	CBSNYT.100686.R19	CBS/NYT	NA	1525	PH	29	OPEN	100	9	9.0	
OCT86	USCBSNYT.103086.R02	CBS/NYT	NA	2016	PH	26	OPEN	105	10	9.5	9.5
NOV86	ESTIMATED										7.3
DEC86	USCBSNYT.86DEC.R03	CBS/NYT	NA	1036	PH	7	OPEN	100	5	5.0	5.0
JAN87	USCBSNYT.87JAN.R04	CBS/NYT	NA	1590	PH	19	OPEN	100	5	5.0	6.9
	USABCWP.87JAN.Q02	ABC/WP	NA	1505	PH	16	OPEN	100	8	8.0	
	USGALLUP.81272.Q04AA	GALLUP	NA	1502	PH	17	OPEN	119	9	7.6	
FEB87	USYANKCS.878607.Q04	YCS	NA	1014	PH	17	OPEN	180	9	5.0	9.7
	USGALNEW.87049.R01	GALLUP	NA	500	PH	5	OPEN	104	15	14.4	
MAR87	CR1STQ87	CAM REP	NA	1405	PR	15	OPEN	100	10	10.0	10.0
APR87	USGALLUP.871274.Q041	GALLUP	NA	1571	PR	11	OPEN	123	11	8.9	8.9
MAY87	USNBCWSJ.132.R17	NBC/WSJ	NA	1568	PH	18	CLOSED	100	13	5.6	5.8
	USGALLUP.TM09PR.R117	GALLUP	NA	4244	PR	2	OPEN	100	6	6.0	
JUN87	CR2NDQ87	CAM REP	NA	1405	PR	15	OPEN	100	10	10.0	10.0
JUL87	ESTIMATED										9.0
AUG87	ESTIMATED										9.0
SEP87	CR3RDQ87	CAM REP	NA	1405	PR	15	OPEN	100	8	8.0	8.0
OCT87	USABCWP.265.R01	ABC/WP	NA	1505	PH	17	OPEN	100	6	6.0	4.5
	USCBSNYT.102787.R04	CBS/NYT	NA	1326	PH	20	OPEN	100	3	3.0	
NOV87	ESTIMATED										6.2
DEC87	CR4THQ87	CAM REP	NA	1405	PR	15	OPEN	100	8	8.0	8.0
JAN88	USYANKCS.884704.Q12	YCS	NA	1804	PH	4	OPEN	179	7	3.9	3.9
FEB88	ESTIMATED										5.4
MAR88	CRISTQ88	CAM REP	NA	1405	PR	15	OPEN	100	7	7.0	7.0
APR88	ESTIMATED										14.0
MAY88	USCBSNYT.88MAY.R04	CBS/NYT	NA	1382	PH	10	OPEN	100	16	16.0	21.0
	USABCWP.299.R02	ABC/WP	NA	1500	PH	22	OPEN	100	26	26.0	
JUN88	CR2NDQ88	CAM REP	NA	1405	PR	15	OPEN	100	16	16.0	16.0

Summary of Public Opinion Surveys (continued)

Date	ID	Co.	Pop	Size	Meth	MP	Form	% Sample	% Survey	% Adjust	% Used
JUL 88	USCBSNYT.071188.R13	CBS/NYT	NA	1177	PH	6	OPEN	100	15	15.0	17.0
	USLAT.158.R13	LA TIMES	NA	2277	PH	7	OPEN	100	19	19.0	
AUG88	USABC.091388	ABC	NA	509	PH	31	OPEN	100	20	20.0	20.0
SEP88	CR3RDQ88	CAM REP	NA	1405	PR	15	OPEN(1,2)	197	35	18.3	18.3
OCT88	ESTIMATED										20.2
NOV88	ESTIMATED										20.2
DEC88	CR4THQ88	CAM REP	NA	1405	PR	15	OPEN	100	22	22.0	22.0
JAN89	USNBCWSJ.011989.R09	NBC/WSJ	NA	2025	PH	15	CLOSED	100	39	16.8	15.9
	USCBSNYT.011989.R06	CBS/NYT	NA	1533	PH	13	OPEN	100	15	15.0	
FEB89	ESTIMATED										19.4
MAR89	CR1STQ89	CAM REP	NA	1405	PR	15	OPEN(1,2)	188	42	22.0	23.0
	USCBS.031689.R02	CBS	NA	663	PH	15	OPEN	100	24	24.0	
APR89	ESTIMATED										25.0
MAY89	USGALLUP.051589.R1	GALLUP	NA	1239	PH	5	OPEN	114	27	27.0	27.0
JUN89	CR2NDQ89	CAM REP	NA	1405	PR	15	OPEN(1,2)	195	39	20.4	20.2
	USNYT.89WOM1.R02	NYT	NA	1497	PH	22	OPEN	100	20	20.0	
JUL89	USCBSNYT.89WOM2.R02	CBS/NYT	NA	978	PH	27	OPEN	100	22	22.0	24.5
	USGALLUP.072489.R1	GALLUP	NA	1247	PH	19	OPEN	100	27	27.0	
AUG89	USABCAP.358.R01	ABC/WP	NA	1509	PH	19	OPEN	100	44	44.0	44.0
SEP89	USCBSNYT.091189.R02	CBS/NYT	NA	824	PH	7	OPEN	100	64	64.0	60.5
	USGALLUP.09128.R01	GALLUP	NA	1238	PH	8	OPEN	108	63	63.0	
	USAPMGEN.28-1.RA01	AP/MG	NA	1071	PH	19	OPEN	100	61	61.0	
	USCBSNYT.092589.R05	CBS/NYT	NA	1347	PH	18	OPEN	100	54	54.0	
OCT89	USABCWP.89OCT.R01	ABC/WP	NA	1620	PH	2	OPEN	100	53	53.0	53.0
NOV89	USGALLUP.111389.R05	GALLUP	NA	1230	PH	10	OPEN	106	38	38.0	38.0
DEC89	ESTIMATED										37.2

Summary of Public Opinion Surveys *(continued)*

Date	ID	Co.	Pop	Size	Meth	MP	Form	% Sample	% Survey	% Adjust	% Used
JAN90	USCBSNYT.90JAN1.R08	CBS/NYT	NA	1557	PH	14	OPEN	100	33	33.0	36.5
	USABCWP.373.R02	ABC/WP	NA	1518	PH	13	OPEN	100	40	40.0	
FEB90	ESTIMATED										35.2
MAR90	USWASHP.908522.R004	WP	NA	1016	PH	24	OPEN	100	34	34.0	34.0
APR90	USWASHP.9091.R01	WP	NA	1003	PH	28	OPEN	100	36	36.0	33.0
	USGALLUP.041190.R01	GALLUP	NA	1223	PH	6	OPEN	100	30	30.0	
MAY90	USPSRA.90TM2A.R101	PRINC	NA	3004	PR	15	OPEN	125	36	28.8	26.4
	USAPMGEN.30-3.RC3	AP/MG	NA	1143	PH	15	OPEN	100	24	24.0	
JUN90	CRJUN89	CAM REP	NA	1405	PR	15	OPEN(1,2)	200	37	19.4	19.4
JUL90	CRJUL89	CAM REP	NA	1405	PR	15	OPEN(1,2)	199	35	18.3	18.2
	USGALLUP.298-1GMP.R10	GALLUP	NA	1242	PH	20	OPEN	100	18	18.0	
AUG90	CRAUG89	CAM REP	NA	1405	PR	15	OPEN(1,2)	193	30	15.7	12.8
	USCBSNYT.082190.R04	CBS/NYT	NA	1422	PH	17	OPEN	100	10	10.0	
SEP90	CRSEP89	CAM REP	NA	1405	PR	15	OPEN(1,2)	199	25	13.1	14.6
	USABCWP.90SEPT.R002	ABC/WP	NA	1011	PH	8	OPEN	100	16	16.0	
OCT90	CROCT89	CAM REP	NA	1405	PR	15	OPEN(1,2)	194	17	8.9	9.6
	USCBSNYT.110390.R05	CBS/NYT	NA	1445	PH	29	OPEN	100	10	10.0	
	USGALLUP.90OCT2.R11	GALLIP	NA	1009	PH	12	OPEN	100	10	10.0	
NOV90	CRNOV89	CAM REP	NA	1405	PR	15	OPEN(1,2)	201	18	9.4	9.4
	USYANKCS.112890.R02	YCS	NA	500	PH	14	CLOSED	100	22	9.5	
DEC90	CRDEC89	CAM REP	NA	1405	PR	15	OPEN(1,2)	199	16	8.4	8.4
JAN91	CRJAN91	CAM REP	NA	1405	PR	15	OPEN(1,2)	201	12	6.3	7.6
	USGALLUP.122011.R04	GALLUP	NA	1006	PH	4	OPEN	100	9	9.0	
FEB91	USGALLUP.020891.R2	GALLUP	NA	1005	PH	1	OPEN	100	5	5.0	5.0
MAR91	USABCWP.429.R01	ABC/WP	NA	1215	PH	2	OPEN	100	11	11.0	10.0
	USCBSNYT.030791.R08	CBS/NYT	NA	1252	PH	5	OPEN	100	10	10.0	
	USGALLUP.031491.R1	GALLUP	NA	1018	PH	8	OPEN	100	11	11.0	
	CRMAR91	CAM REP	NA	1405	PR	15	OPEN(1,2)	200	15	7.9	

Summary of Public Opinion Surveys (continued)

Date	ID	Co.	Pop	Size	Meth	MP	Form	% Sample	% Survey	% Adjust	% Used
APR91	USCBSNYT.040691.R04	CBS/NYT	NA	1283	PH	2	OPEN	100	11	11.0	10.5
	USGALLUP.050491.R1	GALLUP	NA	1005	PH	26	OPEN	100	10	10.0	
MAY91	USLAT.251.R06	LA TIMES	NA	589	PH	6	OPEN	100	16	16.0	13.0
	USGALLUP.061291.R03	GALLUP	NA	1003	PH	24	OPEN	100	10	10.0	
JUN91	USCBSNYT.061091.R04	CBS/NYT	NA	1424	PH	4	OPEN	100	8	8.0	9.0
	USLAT.253.R07	LA TIMES	NA	1439	PH	29	OPEN	100	10	10.0	

Note.

ID = Roper coding for the poll

Co. = Survey organization: Cam Rep = Cambridge Report; NYT = The New York Times; WSJ = Wall Street Journal; YCS = Yankelovich, Clancy and Shulman; WP = Washington Post; LA Times = Los Angeles Times; AP/MG = Associated Press/Media General; Princ = Princeton Survey Research Associates.

Pop = Population (all are national samples of adults)

Size = Sample size

Method = Survey method: Ph = Phone; PR = Personal interview

MP = Midpoint (date of the month) of time period when poll was conducted

Form = Form of question wording: Open; Closed; Open(1,2) first and second choices not separated

% Sample = Total percent of responses in the survey; over 100% due to multiple responses

% Survey = Percent naming drugs as the most important problem

% Adjust = Percent naming drugs as the most important problem after adjustments

% Used = Percent naming drugs as the most important problem used in the time-series analysis

Appendix B: ARIMA Modeling and Analysis

ARIMA IDENTIFICATION, ESTIMATION, AND DIAGNOSIS

The identification phase of ARIMA modeling models these systematic parameters of the stochastic process with the autocorrelation function (ACF) and the partial autocorrelation function (PACF). Every stochastic process has a unique ACF and PACF. The ACF is simply the correlation between the time series and its lags, whereas the PACF is estimated with the Yule–Walker equation system, the explanation of which is beyond the scope of this study (McCain & McCleary, 1979; McCleary & Hay, 1980). In the estimation stage, the parameter estimates must be statistically significant and must lie within the bounds of stationarity and/or invertability. If this is not the case, the model must be identified correctly. After the model has been identified and the parameters are adequately estimated, the model residuals must be diagnosed. The model residuals must be white noise, which is judged by two criteria: (a) the residual ACF must have no spikes at key lags and (b) the Q-statistic (a statistical test for significance in ARIMA modeling) must not be significant. If either criterion is not met, the model must be identified and estimated again.

ARIMA TRANSFER FUNCTIONS, BIVARIATE AND MULTIVARIATE MODELS

ARIMA modeling also allows one to examine statistically significant changes within a series, to examine the relationship between two series, and to build multivariate models for series.

The transfer function shows if a statistically significant change has occurred at a point in time within a series, but it does not explain why the change occurred. The transfer function is modeled as:

Y_t = noise + intervention.

The transfer function can be modeled as a dummy variable, and, as McCain and McCleary (1979) suggested, the transfer function can take one of three forms:
1. Abrupt, constant change (either negative or positive),

$Y_t = \omega I_t$ + noise,

where w is a parameter interpreted as the magnitude of the abrupt, constant change and where the noise is an ARIMA (p,d,q) model that has been identified, estimated, and diagnosed.
2. Gradual, constant change,

$Y_t = \delta Y_{t-1} + \omega I_t$ + noise,

where δ is a parameter to be estimated from the data.
3. Abrupt, temporary change, where the equation is the same as for gradual constant change but It is defined as a pulse change where:

I_t = 0 before the intervention
    = 1 at the moment of the intervention
    = 0 after the intervention.

In addition to bivariate transfer function models, multivariate transfer function relationships between series can also be examined with the use of simultaneous equations (Cuddington, 1980; Dearing, 1989; Rogers et al., 1991). The approach is similar to the simultaneous equations used by Behr and Iyenger (1985); however, ARIMA modeling is used to model the series and then ARIMA transfer function procedures are used to examine the relationship between the series.

ARIMA modeling can also be used in other approaches to examine the relationship between two series. One primary use is concomitant variation; that is, to introduce an independent time series for the purpose of reducing background noise (or unexplained variance) in a dependent-variable time series (McCleary & Hay, 1980). The other use is to model the relationship between two series with the ARIMA cross-correlation function to address the issue of causality between two series (Gonzenbach, 1992; McCleary & Hay, 1980). Two approaches are possible in this cross-correlation ARIMA analysis. One is to model the dependent series with ARIMA modeling and then use this as a filter (or prewhitener) to model the independent series before the cross-lagged correlations are examined (McCleary & Hay, 1980). Another approach, the (1977) Haugh–Box method, models each series independently with ARIMA modeling and then uses the cross-correlation function to determine their relationship over time (Mark, 1979; Vandaele, 1983). Also, the relationship between two series can be examined with the use of regression techniques using Yule–Walker estimation. The models are identified, estimated, and diagnosed. Then the modeled series are examined with Yule–Walker estimation (SAS Institute, 1988).

Finally, ARIMA modeling can be used to examine multivariate models that address the effect of several independent series on a dependent-variable series, all of which have been prewhitened (McCleary & Hay, 1980; Rogers et al., 1991). As with the bivariate analysis, Yule–Walker estimation can be used for this multivariate analysis (SAS Institute, 1988).

References

Adams, E. H., Blanken, A. J., Ferguson, L. D., & Kopstein, A. (1990). *Overview of selected drug trends.* Rockville, MD: National Institute on Drug Abuse.

After a rough start, Nancy Reagan attaining influence and respect. (1985, January 14). *Time,* p. 24.

Barrett, P. M. (1990, November 19). Though the drug war isn't over, spotlight turns to other issues. *Wall Street Journal,* p. 1.

Baumgartner, F. R., & Jones, B. D. (1993). *Agendas and instability in American politics.* Chicago: The University of Chicago Press.

Behr, R. L., & Iyengar, S. (1985). Television news, real-world cues, and changes in the public agenda. *Public Opinion Quarterly, 49,* 38–57.

Beniger, J. R. (1978). Media content as social indicators: The Greenfield index of agenda-setting. *Communication Research, 5,* 437–451.

Box, G. E., & Jenkins, G. M. (1976). *Time series analysis: Forecasting and control* (rev. ed.). San Francisco: Holden-Day.

Brosius, H.-B., & Kepplinger, H. M. (1990a). The agenda-setting function of television news: Static and dynamic views. *Communication Research, 17,* 183–211.

Brosius, H.-B., & Kepplinger, H. M. (1990b, June). *Linear and nonlinear models of agenda-setting in television.* Paper presented to the 40th Annual Convention of the International Communication Association, Dublin, Ireland.

Converse, P. E. (1987). Changing conceptions of public opinion in the political process. *Public Opinion Quarterly, 51,* S12–S24.

Cutlip, S. M. (1962, May 26). Third of newspapers' content PR-inspired. *Editor and Publisher,* p. 68.

Cuddington, J. T. (1980). Simultaneous-equations test of the natural rate and other classical hypotheses. *Journal of Political Economy, 88,* 539–549.

Dearing, J. W. (1989). Setting the polling agenda for the issue of AIDS. *Public Opinion Quarterly, 53,* 309–329.

Downs, A. (1972). Up and down with ecology—The "issue-attention cycle." *Public Interest, 28,* 28–50.

Erbring, L., Goldenberg, E. N., & Miller, A. H. (1980). Front-page news and real-world cues. *American Journal of Political Science, 24,* 16–49.

Eyal, C. H. (1979). *Time-frame in agenda-setting research: A study of the conceptual and methodological factors affecting the time frame context of the agenda-setting process.* Unpublished doctoral dissertation, Syracuse University, Syracuse, NY.

Funkhouser, G. R. (1973). The issues of the sixties: An exploratory study of the dynamics of public opinion. *Public Opinion Quarterly, 37,* 62–75.

Gilberg, S., Eyal, C., McCombs, M. E., & Nichols, D. (1980). The state of the union address and the press agenda. *Journalism Quarterly, 52,* 15–22.

Gilbert, R. E. (1981). Television and presidential power. *Journal of Social, Political and Economic Studies, 6,* 75–93.

Gonzenbach, W. J. (1992). A time-series analysis of the drug issue, 1985–1990: The press, the president and public opinion. *International Journal of Public Opinion Research, 4,* 126–147.

Granger, C. W. J. (1980). Testing for causality: A personal viewpoint. *Journal of Economic Dynamics and Control, 2,* 329–352.

Haugh, L. D., & Box, G. E. P. (1977). Identification of dynamic regression (distributed lag) models connecting two time series. *Journal of the American Statistical Association, 72,* 121–130.

Hilgartner, S., & Bosk, C. L. (1988). The rise and fall of social problems: A public arenas model. *American Journal of Sociology, 94,* 53–78.

Holsti, O. (1969). *Content analysis for the social science and humanities.* Reading, MA: Addison-Wesley.

Iyengar, S., & Kinder, D. R. (1987). *News that matters: Television and American opinion.* Chicago: The University of Chicago Press.

Johnston, L. D. (1989). America's drug problem in the media: Is it real or is it Memorex? In P. J. Shoemaker (Ed.), *Communication campaigns about drugs: Government, media and the public* (pp. 97–112). Hillsdale, NJ: Lawrence Erlbaum Associates.

Kepplinger, H. M., Donsbach, W., Brosius, H.-B., & Staab, J. F. (1989). Media tone and public opinion: A longitudinal study of media coverage and public opinion on Chancellor Kohl. *International Journal of Public Opinion Research, 1,* 326–342.

Kerr, P. (1986, November 17). Anatomy of an issue: Drugs, the evidence, the reaction. *The New York Times,* p. 1.

Kessler, R. C., & Greenberg, D. F. (1981). *Linear panel analysis: Models of quantitative change.* New York: Academic Press.

Klapper, J. T. (1960). *The effects of mass communication.* New York: Free Press.

Lachter, S. B., & Forman, A. (1989). Drug abuse in the United States. In Pamela J. Shoemaker (Ed.), *Communication campaigns about drugs: Government, media and the public* (pp. 7–12). Hillsdale, NJ: Lawrence Erlbaum Associates.

Leff, D. R., Protess, D. L., & Brooks, S. C. (1986). Crusading journalism: Changing public attitudes and policy-making. *Public Opinion Quarterly, 50,* 300–315.

Lichter, R. S., & Lichter, L. S. (1989, January). The war on drugs: Covering the continuing debate over drug abuse. *Media Monitor,* pp. 1–6.

Lichter, R. S., & Lichter, L. S. (1990, October). Bush's war on drugs: Covering the continuing debate over drug abuse. *Media Monitor,* pp. 1–6.

Lippmann, W. (1922). *Public opinion.* New York: Macmillian.

MacKuen, M. B. (1981). Social communication and the mass policy agenda. In M. B. MacKuen & S. L. Coombs (Eds.), *More than news: Media power in public affairs* (pp. 19–144), Newbury Park, CA: Sage.

Mark, M. M. (1979). Inferring cause from passive observation. In T. D. Cook & D. T. Campbell (Eds.), *Quasi-experimentation: Design & analysis issues for field settings* (pp. 295–340). Boston: Houghton Mifflin.

Markus, G. B. (1979). *Analyzing panel data.* Beverly Hills, CA: Sage.

McCain, L. J., & McCleary, R. (1979). The statistical analysis of the simple interrupted time-series quasi-experiment. In T. D. Cook & D. T. Campbell (Eds.), *Quasi-experimentation: Design & analysis issues for field settings* (pp. 233–294). Boston: Houghton Mifflin.

McCleary, R., & Hay, R. A. (1980). *Applied times series analysis for the social sciences.* Beverly Hills, CA: Sage.

McCombs, M. E. (1993). *The continuing evolution of agenda setting research.* Seoul: Korean Press Institute.

McCombs, M. E., Einsiedel, E., & Weaver, D. (1991). *Contemporary public opinion: Issues and the news.* Hillsdale, NJ: Lawrence Erlbaum Associates.

McCombs, M. E., & Shaw, D. L. (1972). The agenda-setting function of mass media. *Public Opinion Quarterly, 36,* 176–184.

McLeod, J. M., Becker L. B., & Byrnes, J. E. (1974). Another look at the agenda-setting function of the press. *Communication Research, 1,* 131–166.

Merriam, J. E. (1989). National media coverage of drug issues, 1983–1987. In P. J. Shoemaker (Ed.), *Communication campaigns about drugs: Government, media, and the public* (pp. 21–29). Hillsdale, NJ: Lawrence Erlbaum Associates.

Molotch, H. L., Protess, D. L., & Gordon, M. T. (1987). The media-policy connection: Ecologies of news. In D. Paletz (Ed.), *Political communication: Theories, cases and assessments* (pp. 26–48). Norwood, NJ: Ablex.

Munn, G. G., Garcia, F. L., & Woelfel, C. J. (1991). *Encyclopedia of business and finance* (9th ed.). Rolling Meadows, IL: Bankers Publishing Company.

Neuman, W. R. (1990). The threshold of public attention. *Public Opinion Quarterly, 54,* 159–176.

Neuman, W. R., Just, M., & Crigler, A. (1988, June). *Knowledge, opinion, and the news: The calculus of political learning.* Paper presented at the annual meeting of the American Political Science Association, Washington, DC.

Office of National Drug Control Strategy. (1991, February) . *National drug control strategy: Budget summary.* Washington, DC: White House.

O'Keefe, G. J. (1985). "Taking a bite out of crime": The impact of a public information campaign. *Communication Research, 12,* 147–178.

Ostrom, C. W. (1990). *Time series analysis: Regression techniques* (2nd ed.). Beverly Hills, CA: Sage.

The other war.(1990, December 8–14). *The Economist,* pp. 13–14.

Reese, S. D., & Danielian, L. H. (1989). Intermedia influences and the drug issue: Converging on cocaine. In P. J. Shoemaker (Ed.), *Communication campaigns about drugs: Government, media and the public* (pp. 29–46). Hillsdale, NJ: Lawrence Erlbaum Associates.

Rogers, E. M., & Dearing, J. W. (1988). Agenda-setting research: Where it has been, where is it going? In J. A. Anderson (Ed.), *Communication Yearbook 11* (pp. 555–594). Newbury Park, CA: Sage.

Rogers, E. M., Dearing, J. W., & Chang, S. (1991, April). AIDS in the 1980s: The agenda-setting process of a public issue. *Journalism Monographs, 126.*

SAS Institute (1988). *SAS/stat user's guide, release 6.03 Ed.* Cary, NC: Author.

Schuman, H., & Scott, J. (1987). Problems in the use of survey questions to measure public opinion. *Science, 236,* 957–959.

Scott, W. (1955). Reliability in content analysis: A case of nominal scale coding. *Public Opinion Quarterly, 17,* 321–325.

Shannon, E. (1990, December 3). A losing battle. *Time,* pp. 44–48.

Shaw, D. L. (1977). The press agenda in a community setting. In M. E. McCombs & D. L. Shaw (Eds.), *The agenda-setting function of the press: The emergence of American political issues* (pp. 19–31). St. Paul, MN: West.

Shaw, D. L., & McCombs, M. E. (1977). *The agenda-setting function of the press: The emergence of American political issues.* St. Paul, MN: West.

Shaw, D. L., & McCombs, M. E. (1989). Dealing with illicit drugs: The power—and limits—of mass media agenda setting. In P. J. Shoemaker (Ed.), *Communication campaigns about drugs: Government, media and the public* (pp. 113–120). Hillsdale, NJ: Lawrence Erlbaum Associates.

Shoemaker, P. J., Wanta, W., & Leggett, D. (1989). Drug coverage and public opinion, 1972–1986. In P. J. Shoemaker (Ed.), *Communication campaigns about drugs: Government, media and the public* (pp. 67–80). Hillsdale, NJ: Lawrence Erlbaum Associates.

Sims, C. (1972). Money, income, and causality. *American Economic Review, 62,* 540–552.

Smith, K. A. (1987). Effects of newspaper coverage on community issue concerns and local government. *Communication Research, 14,* 379–395.

Smith, T. (1980). America's most important problems—a trend analysis, 1946–1976. *Public Opinion Quarterly, 44,* 164–180.

Sohn, A. B. (1978). A longitudinal analysis of local non-political agenda-setting effects. *Journalism Quarterly, 55,* 325–333.

Steadman, H. J., & Cocozza, J. (1977). Selective reporting and the public's misconceptions of the criminally insane. *Public Opinion Quarterly, 41,* 523–533.

Stone, G. C., & McCombs, M. E. (1981). Tracing the time lag in agenda-setting. *Journalism Quarterly, 58,* 151–155.

Sullivan, L. W. (1990, December 19). *Release on the national household survey on drug abuse.* Rockville, MD: National Institute on Drug Abuse.

Tedrow, L. M., & Mahoney, E. R. (1979). Trends in attitudes toward abortion: 1972–1976. *Public Opinion Quarterly, 43,* 181–189.

Tipton, L., Haney, R. D., & Basehart, J. R. (1975). Media agenda-setting in city and state election campaigns. *Journalism Quarterly, 52,* 15–22.

Turk, J. V. (1985). Information subsidies and influence. *Public Relations Review, 11,* 1–14.

Turk, J. V. (1986a, December). Information subsidies and media content. *Journalism Monographs, 100.*

Turk, J. V. (1986b, Summer). Public relations influence on the news. *Newspaper Research Journal,* pp. 15–27.

Vandaele, W. (1983). *Applied time series and Box–Jenkins models.* Orlando, FL: Academic Press.

Wanta, W., Stephenson, M. A., Turk, J. V., & McCombs, M. E. (1989). How president's state of union talks influenced news media agendas. *Journalism Quarterly, 66,* 537–541.

Watt, J. H., & van den Berg, S. A. (1978). Time series analysis of alternative media effects theories. In B. D. Reuben (Ed.), *Communication yearbook 2* (pp. 215–224). New Brunswick, NJ: Transaction Books.

Watt, J. H., & van den Berg, S. A. (1981). How time dependency influences media effects in a community controversy. *Journalism Quarterly, 58,* 43–50.

Weaver, D. H. (1980). Audience need for orientation and media effects. *Communication Research, 7,* 361–376.

Weaver, D. H. (1987). Media agenda-setting and elections: Assumptions and implications. In David L. Paletz (Ed.), *Political communication research: Approaches, studies, and assessments* (pp. 176–191). Norwood, NJ: Ablex.

Weaver, D. H., Graber, D. A., McCombs, M. E., & Eyal, C. H. (1981). *Media agenda-setting in a presidential election: Issues, images, and interest.* New York: Praeger.

Winter, J. P., & Eyal, C. H. (1981). Agenda setting for the civil rights issue. *Public Opinion Quarterly, 45,* 376–383.

Yagade, A., & Dozier, D. M. (1990). The media agenda-setting effect of concrete versus abstract issues. *Journalism Quarterly, 67,* 3–10.

Zhu, J. (1992). Issue competition and attention distraction: A zero-sum theory of agenda-setting. *Journalism Quarterly, 68,* 825–836.

Zucker, H. G. (1978). The variable nature of news media influence. In B. Reuben (Ed.), *Communication yearbook 2* (pp. 225–240). New Brunswick, NJ: Transaction Books.

Author Index

Subject Index

For Product Safety Concerns and Information please contact our EU
representative GPSR@taylorandfrancis.com Taylor & Francis Verlag GmbH,
Kaufingerstraße 24, 80331 München, Germany

Printed and bound by CPI Group (UK) Ltd, Croydon, CR0 4YY
01/05/2025
01858367-0001